Nigeria:

Malaria Operational Plan FY 2014

Table of Contents

ABBREVIATIONS

ACSM	Advocacy, Communication and Social Mobilization
ACT	Artemisinin-based combination therapy
AMFm	Affordable Medicines Facility for malaria
ANC	Antenatal care clinic
BCC	Behavior change communication
CDC	U.S. Centers for Disease Control and Prevention
DDIC	Direct Delivery and Information Capture
DfID	United Kingdom Department for International Development
DHS	Demographic and Health Survey
DOD	U.S. Department of Defense
EPI	Expanded Program on Immunization
EUV	End-use verification
FANC	Focused antenatal care
FELTP	Field Epidemiology and Laboratory Training Program
FY	Fiscal year
GHI	Global Health Initiative
Global Fund	Global Fund to Fight AIDS, Tuberculosis, and Malaria
GoN	Government of Nigeria
HMIS	Health Management Information System
IPC	Interpersonal communication
IPTp	Intermittent preventive treatment for pregnant women
IRS	Indoor residual spraying
ITN	Insecticide-treated net
LGA	Local Government Authority
MAPS	Malaria Action Program for States
MDG	Millennium Development Goal
MICS	Multiple indicator cluster survey
MIP	Malaria in pregnancy
MIS	Malaria Indicator Survey
MNCH	Maternal, Newborn and Child Health
MOH	Ministry of Health
MOP	Malaria Operational Plan
NAFDAC	National Agency for Food and Drug Administration and Control
NMCP	National Malaria Control Program
PEPFAR	U.S. President's Emergency Plan for AIDS Relief
PMI	U.S. President's Malaria Initiative
PMVs	Patent medicine vendors

QA	Quality assurance
QC	Quality control
RBM	Roll Back Malaria
RDT	Rapid diagnostic test
SFH	Society for Family Health
SMCP	State Malaria Control Program
SP	Sulfadoxine-pyrimethamine
SuNMaP	Support for the National Malaria Program
TSHIP	Targeted State High Impact Project
UNICEF	United Nations Children's Fund
USAID	United States Agency for International Development
USG	United States Government
WHO	World Health Organization
WRP	Walter Reed Program

I. EXECUTIVE SUMMARY

Malaria prevention and control are major foreign assistance objectives of the U.S. Government (USG). In May 2009, President Barack Obama announced the Global Health Initiative (GHI), a multi-year, comprehensive effort to reduce the burden of disease and promote healthy communities and families around the world. Through the GHI, the United States is helping partner countries improve health outcomes, with a particular focus on improving the health of women, newborns, and children.

The President's Malaria Initiative (PMI) is a core component of the GHI, along with Human Immunodeficiency Virus/Acquired Immunodeficiency Syndrome (HIV/AIDS), and tuberculosis. PMI was launched in June 2005 as a five-year, $1.2 billion initiative to rapidly scale up malaria prevention and treatment interventions and reduce malaria-related mortality by 50% in 15 high-burden countries in sub-Saharan Africa. With passage of the 2008 Lantos-Hyde Act, funding for PMI was extended and, as part of the GHI, the goal of PMI was adjusted to reduce malaria-related mortality by 70% in the original 15 countries by the end of 2015. Expansion was authorized to additional PMI countries, including Nigeria, the Democratic Republic of Congo and up to seven additional high-burden countries. The goal for any new countries added after the initial 15 is to achieve a 50% reduction in malaria-related mortality in at-risk population by 2015 as compared with 2009-2010 baseline levels. These goals will be achieved by reaching 85% coverage of the most vulnerable groups – children under five years of age (under five) and pregnant women – with proven preventive and therapeutic interventions, including artemisinin-based combination therapies (ACTs), insecticide-treated nets (ITNs), intermittent preventive treatment for pregnant women (IPTp), and indoor residual spraying (IRS).

With a population of about 172 million and reporting more deaths due to malaria than any country in the world, Nigeria became the seventeenth PMI country in 2010. Malaria accounts for 60% of outpatient visits and 30% of hospitalizations among children under five in Nigeria. The Demographic and Health Survey (DHS) 2008 reported an infant mortality of 75 per 1000 live births and an under five mortality of 157 per 1000 live births in the preceding five-year period. Impressive progress has been made in malaria control efforts in recent years. The proportion of households owning one or more ITNs increased from just 8% in the DHS 2008 to 42% in the Malaria Indicator Survey (MIS) 2010, and the proportion of children under five reported to have slept under an ITN the night before the survey increased from 6% in the DHS 2008 to 29% in the MIS 2010.

Donor support to malaria control in Nigeria has increased dramatically in recent years. Nigeria was the recipient of a $600 million Global Fund to Fight AIDS, Tuberculosis, and Malaria (Global Fund) Round 8 award that was signed in 2008. Phase II of this grant, which started in August 2012, has a total approved amount of $150 million. Combined with the last six months of funds in the Phase I grant, the total budget for the full three-year period of Phase II, from 1 November 2011 until 31 October 2014, is $225 million. Nigeria was also one of nine countries to pilot the Affordable Medicines Facility-malaria (AMFm). The goal of AMFm was to reduce the retail price of ACTs to a point that they are as affordable as many of the cheapest antimalarial monotherapies. The pilot activities are now being transitioned to full integration under the Global Fund. In 2009, a second phase of the World Bank Malaria Booster Program provided $100 million in addition to the original commitment of $180 million to support a broad set of malaria interventions in seven states. The Booster Program ended in June 2013, but the country has requested a no cost extension of the project to June 2014. The United Kingdom Department for International Development (DfID) launched a five-year £50 million (about $80 million) malaria program in 2008. Currently, the program is in a period of no cost extension, but DfID has indicated a willingness to maintain funding at similar levels for 2014 and 2015.

Nigeria's large population and decentralized system make it virtually impossible for one donor to provide meaningful assistance to the entire population. The National Malaria Control Program (NMCP) works with donors to ensure that the six geopolitical zones, 36 states, and the Federal Capital Territory of Abuja receive support proportional to the burden of malaria and the level of donor assistance, and that assistance is spread to reach as many states as possible. The United States Agency for International Development (USAID) has funded malaria activities in Nigeria over the past decade. When Nigeria became a PMI country with fiscal year (FY) 2011 funding, it received $43.6 million. The final FY 2012 and FY 2013 budgets were $60.1 million. The FY 2014 PMI Operational Plan for Nigeria was developed during a planning visit carried out in April 2013 with USAID and the Centers for Disease Control and Prevention (CDC) headquarters' and field staff and leadership of the NMCP. The team obtained input from all key national and international partners involved in malaria prevention and control in the country. The PMI plan supports the National Malaria Strategic Plan 2009-2013 and is coordinated with national and international partners to complement overall funding and resources. In FY 2014 the program will continue to focus on eleven states: Akwa Ibom, Bauchi, Cross River, Kebbi, Nasarawa, Sokoto, Zamfara, Benue, Ebonyi, Oyo and Kogi. With FY 2014 funding, PMI will support a comprehensive package of malaria interventions to reach an estimated population of about 50 million in those eleven of the 36 Nigerian states. The FY 2014 budget is $60.1 million.

Insecticide-Treated Nets (ITNs): The National Malaria Strategic Plan 2009-2013 calls for universal coverage of ITNs, defined as two ITNs per household, by the end of 2010. This was reviewed in 2011 by the in-country Roll Back Malaria (RBM) team and changed to align with the World Health Organization (WHO) recommendation of one long-lasting insecticide-treated net (ITN) for every two persons and using a 1:1.8 ratio for quantification of needs to reach the 1:2 target. Nigeria required about 64 million ITNs to reach the original universal coverage goal of two ITNs per household nationwide, but shortfalls in donations mean that the total available for delivery is about 54 million and as of May 2013, about 50 million ITNs had been distributed through mass campaigns to 34 of Nigeria's 36 states and the Federal Capital Territory of Abuja.

Major contributors to this national effort include Global Fund, World Bank, UNITAID, United Nations Children's Fund (UNICEF), DfID, PMI, and Canadian Red Cross.

The MIS 2010 revealed significant improvement in net coverage and use following these mass campaigns, while the Multiple Indicator Cluster Survey (MICS) 2011 appeared to show some decrease. The MIS 2010 found that 59% of children under five in households with at least one ITN slept under a net the previous night as compared with 50% in the DHS 2008. The increase among pregnant women was greater, to 34% in 2010 from 5% in 2008 among all pregnant women and to 66% in 2010 from 45% in 2008 among those in households with at least one ITN. The MICS 2011 reported only 33% of children under five in households with at least one ITN slept under a net the previous night, and 35% of pregnant women in households with a net. The differences may largely be explained by seasonality: the MIS 2010 was conducted during the rainy season when ITN use is expected to be highest, while the MICS 2011 was conducted during the dry season.

With FY 2014 funding, PMI will focus on providing ITNs through various channels to maintain high coverage, or to at least prevent further declines in the PMI focus states. PMI will procure and distribute approximately 5 million ITNs that will support mass campaigns in three states and continuous distribution in six other states. Channels for distributing ITNs outside of campaigns will include antenatal care (ANC) and vaccination clinics, and possibly through additional channels such as schools or community-based distribution based on the results of pilot programs. PMI's goal is to maintain 90% ownership of ITNs in the 11 PMI focus states.

Indoor Residual Spraying (IRS): The Nigerian National Malaria Strategic Plan 2009-2013 calls for scale-up of IRS to cover 20% of all households in Nigeria, or about 7 million households, by the end of 2013. The World Bank supported IRS in seven states with PMI participating in two local government authorities (LGAs) of Nasarawa State, covering approximately 65,000 structures and protecting a population of over 300,000 in 2011 and 2012. With FY 2013 funding, PMI shifted funding from an IRS-intense focus to an NMCP-led national surveillance program for vector bionomics and insecticide resistance monitoring, while supporting IRS advocacy and training. PMI seeks to transition IRS spray operations to the state and/or local government, while continuing to assist the NMCP to update its IRS strategy and train staff on IRS. With FY 2014 funding, PMI will support the NMCP to establish entomologic surveillance sites in each of the six geopolitical zones to monitor vector susceptibility to WHO-approved IRS insecticides. Training and equipment support will build capacity for entomological expertise at the federal and state levels.

Intermittent Preventive Treatment for Pregnant Women (IPTp): Scale-up of IPTp continues to be a challenge in Nigeria. According to the DHS 2008, only 58% of pregnant women had access to ANC from a skilled provider and 62% of pregnant women delivered at home. Five percent of pregnant women received two or more of the recommended doses of IPTp, with an increase to 13% in the MIS 2010. A number of factors contribute to the low uptake of IPTp including sporadic availability of sulfadoxine-pyrimethamine (SP), low ANC clinic attendance, and poor quality of ANC service delivery.

To address these issues, with FY 2013 funding, PMI procured SP for IPTp as a part of focused ANC in its 11 focus states. PMI also provided technical assistance at the federal and state levels to update the malaria in pregnancy (MIP) policy and strategic plan per WHO guidance, review and update the MIP training manuals, train health workers, and provide job aids on IPTp. PMI will continue this support with FY 2014 funding, with an increased focus on ANC services in hard-to-reach communities. Though it will procure SP for IPTp in the 11 states, PMI will advocate for those states to use their own budgets in the future to procure this inexpensive drug for IPTp.

Case Management: Malaria case management in Nigeria is weak, suffering from a general absence of diagnostics, a weak supply chain system, and poor delivery of services at the public health facility level. The MIS 2010 revealed that of those children who received malaria treatment, only 12% took an ACT while 57% took chloroquine and 22% took SP. In addition, only 5% of children under five with fever had their blood tested for malaria.

The NMCP updated the National Guidelines for Diagnosis and Treatment of Malaria, aligning it with WHO's revised recommendations on universal diagnostic testing for malaria from 2010. The NMCP is working with the states to improve the delivery of malaria case management by implementing new guidelines and improving supportive supervision. However, the lack of rapid diagnostic tests (RDTs) delayed the rollout of expanded malaria diagnostics. PMI-procured RDTs began arriving in mid-2012 for use in primary and secondary public health facilities. The challenge is to build trust in the RDT results among health care providers. PMI-supported training of laboratory scientists in six states continues in collaboration with the Nigerian Ministry of Defense and the U.S. Department of Defense (DOD)-Walter Reed Program on malaria diagnosis. PMI complemented this national-level instruction through state and LGA training and supervision on the appropriate use of RDTs and microscopy. Plans are now to begin to extend diagnostics to the private sector and community levels.

Case management is hampered by the disjointed public sector procurement, supply, and distribution system that leads to stockouts of essential commodities including first-line ACTs. With the problems plaguing public sector health service delivery, it is not surprising that only 30% of Nigerians seek fever care from these facilities. Nigeria piloted the AMFm, reducing the ACT price in the private sector. With AMFm transitioning to the Global Fund in 2013, the NMCP and RBM partners are exploring options for continuing a private sector subsidy for ACTs.

With FY 2014 funding, PMI will procure RDTs to support scale up of laboratory diagnosis in its 11 focus states and to expand into the private sector. Support for training of health and laboratory workers will proceed at the national, state, LGA, and community levels, in both the public and private sectors. Technical guidance will be provided to develop and implement a comprehensive quality assurance/quality control program. Strengthening pharmaceutical and commodity management systems at the state level and below, ideally to the facility level, will continue as a PMI priority, with support to improving forecasting, management, and distribution, along with capacity building for drug quality control. Finally, PMI will procure ACTs and drugs for severe malaria in its 11 focus states. Training and supervision on malaria case management will target not only health workers in public health facilities but also private sector patent medicine vendors in selected LGAs.

Advocacy, Communication and Social Mobilization: Nigeria's updated National Malaria Advocacy, Communication and Social Mobilization Strategic Framework and Implementation Plan recommends various channels of communication based on the target audiences. Malaria educational messages generally reach households using radio, community drama, printed materials, community and religious leaders, and through community support groups and household visits of volunteers as interpersonal communication. PMI supports behavior change communication as a cross-cutting activity in all key malaria interventions. Specific activities include increasing and improving the information delivered by facility-based and community health workers, transmitting malaria educational messages in local languages through radio, and using community volunteers for interpersonal communication. PMI also continues to promote the updated National Advocacy Kit to harmonize malaria educational messages.

Monitoring and Evaluation: The PMI Nigeria plan includes a strong monitoring and evaluation component to identify and correct problems in program implementation and measure progress against goals and targets. In the 11 focus states, PMI is strengthening the harmonized Health Management Information System (HMIS) so that routine malaria data is more accurate and reliable from the health facility level to the state level, and that this information is analyzed and used for planning and decision-making. Harmonized HMIS tools as well as a Logistics Management Information System for malaria commodities are now being implemented, with PMI supporting the instructional manual and training of trainers. The PMI is also supporting the Nigeria DHS 2013 and the national MIS planned for 2014. To build capacity in monitoring and evaluation within the NMCP and state malaria programs, PMI will support the training of Fellows in the Nigeria Field Epidemiology and Laboratory Training Program, in collaboration with CDC.

II. STRATEGY

1. Introduction

The United States Agency for International Development (USAID) has been supporting malaria control efforts in Nigeria for more than ten years. The level of USAID malaria funding increased to about $7 million annually in fiscal year (FY) 2007 and FY 2008, and then more than doubled to about $16 million in FY 2009 and FY 2010. In FY 2011, Nigeria's first year as a President's Malaria Initiative (PMI) country, the funding for Nigeria was $43.5 million and in FY 2012 and FY 2013 the original budget figures, $43.2 million, were increased to $60.1 million and $73.271 million respectively.

Global Health Initiative and PMI

Malaria prevention and control is a major foreign assistance objective of the United States Government (USG). In May 2009, President Barack Obama announced the Global Health Initiative (GHI), a multi-year, comprehensive effort to reduce the burden of disease and promote healthy communities and families around the world. Through the GHI, the United States helps partner countries improve health outcomes, with a particular focus on improving the health of women, newborns and children. The GHI is a global commitment to invest in healthy and productive lives, building upon and expanding the USG's successes in addressing specific diseases and issues.

Malaria prevention and control is a core component of the GHI, along with programs to address HIV/AIDS and tuberculosis. PMI was launched in June 2005 as a five-year, $1.2 billion initiative to rapidly scale up malaria prevention and treatment interventions and reduce malaria-related mortality by 50% in 15 high-burden countries in sub-Saharan Africa. With passage of the 2008 Lantos-Hyde Act, funding for PMI was extended through FY 2014 and, as part of the GHI, PMI's goal was adjusted to reduce malaria-related mortality by 70% in the original 15 countries by the end of 2015. The act called for an expansion of PMI to additional countries such as Nigeria, Democratic Republic of Congo and at most seven other high-burden countries. In 2010 and 2011, expansion countries included Nigeria, DRC, Guinea and Zimbabwe. The goal for these new countries is to achieve a 50% reduction in malaria-related mortality in the at-risk population by 2015 as compared with 2009-2010 baseline levels. These goals will be achieved by reaching 85% coverage of the most vulnerable groups – children under five years of age (under five) and pregnant women – with proven preventive and therapeutic interventions, including artemisinin-based combination therapies (ACTs), insecticide-treated nets (ITNs), intermittent preventive treatment for pregnant women (IPTp), and indoor residual spraying (IRS).

In implementing this initiative, the U.S. Government (USG) is committed to working closely with host governments and within existing national malaria control plans. Efforts are coordinated with other national and international partners, including the Global Fund to Fight AIDS, Tuberculosis, and Malaria (Global Fund), Roll Back Malaria (RBM), United Kingdom Department for International Development (DfID), the World Bank Malaria Booster Program, and the non-governmental and private sectors, to ensure that investments are complementary and that RBM and Millennium Development Goals (MDGs) are achieved. Country planning and evaluation activities for PMI are highly consultative and held in collaboration with the National Malaria Control Program (NMCP) and other partners.

This FY 2014 Malaria Operational Plan (MOP) presents a detailed implementation plan for Nigeria's fourth year as a PMI country and is strongly aligned with the NMCP's Strategic Plan 2009-2013 (also called the National Malaria Strategic Plan 2009-2013). The MOP was developed in close consultation with the NMCP leadership and with input from all key national and international partners for malaria control and prevention in Nigeria. The MOP briefly

Figure 1: PMI Focus states, Nigeria, Fiscal Year 2014

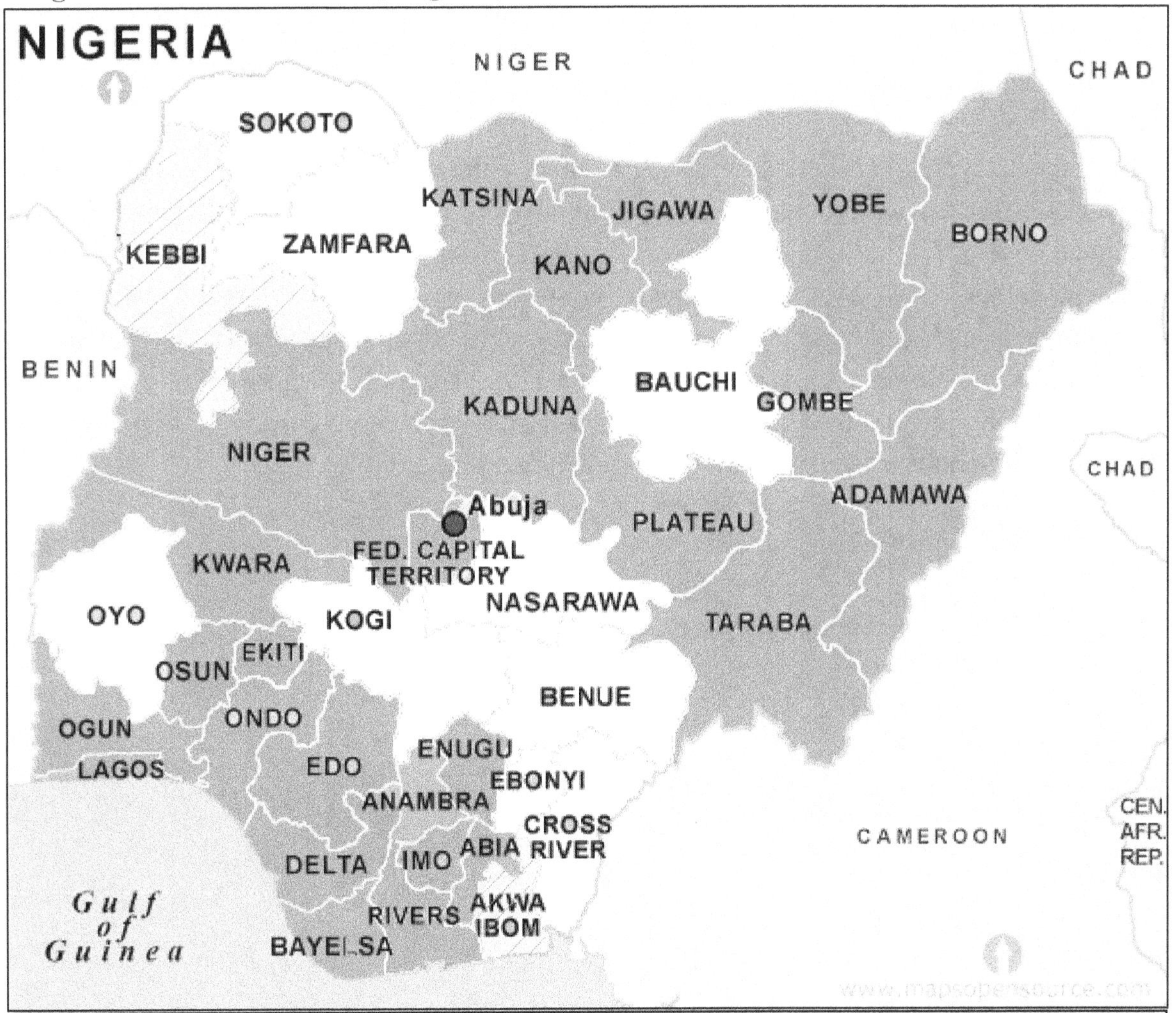

Legend: White colored states are the nine PMI focus states prior to the FY 2014 MOP. The two states with strips, Akwa Ibom and Kebbi, were added in the FY 2014 MOP.

reviews the current status of malaria control, prevention policies, interventions, and identifies challenges and unmet needs to achieve PMI goals. This document was developed during a visit to Nigeria by USAID and Centers for Disease Control and Prevention (CDC) staff in April/May 2013. Due to the large population at risk of malaria in Nigeria and the strong support of other donors, PMI focuses activities on 11 states selected in consultation with the NMCP, reaching an estimated population of about 50 million at risk of malaria.

The PMI FY 2014 budget for Nigeria is currently set at $60.1 million. Note that the final FY 2013 Congressional appropriation for PMI permitted an increase in Nigeria's original allocation of $60.1 million to a revised country budget of $73.271 million. Among other things, these additional funds were used to extend coverage of PMI support to two new states, selected in consultation with the NMCP, and to expand operational activities though existing and new partners. The FY 2014 MOP describes continued support to all 11 states despite the lower budget level. The PMI team is optimistic that the final FY 2014 appropriations will ultimately allow a similar level of PMI support for expanded geographic coverage and operational activities that it provided in FY 2013.

2. Nigeria malaria situation

Nigeria is the most populous country in Africa with an estimated annual growth rate of about 2.6% and an estimated total population of approximately 172 million for 2014. It comprises six geopolitical zones, 36 states (plus the Federal Capital Territory of Abuja), and 774 local government authorities (LGAs), each with an average population of about 200,000 residents (Figure 1). Each state has an elected governor, an executive council, and a house of assembly with the power to make state laws. State governments have substantial autonomy and exercise considerable authority over the allocation and utilization of their resources, limiting the influence of the federal government over state and local government affairs.

Figure 2: Map of Nigeria with geopolitical zones

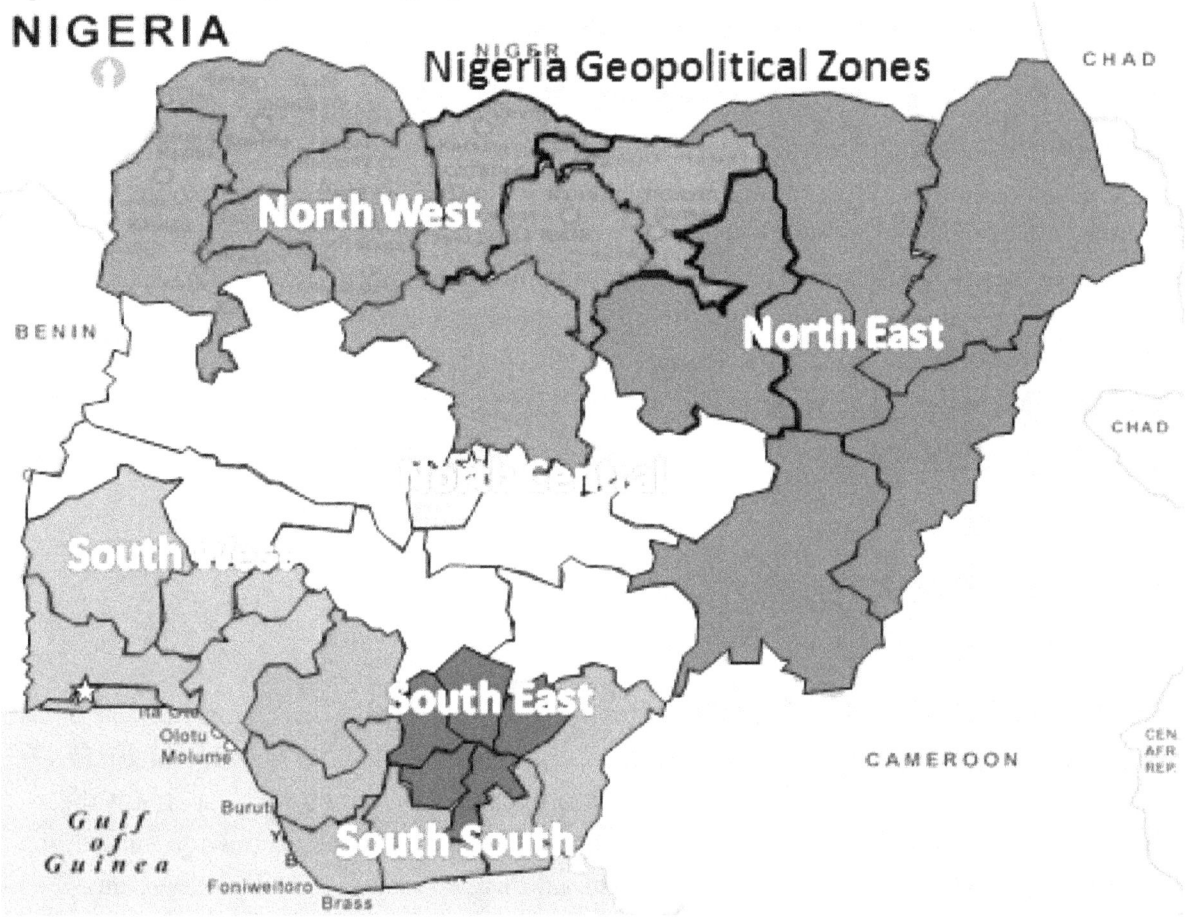

Nigeria is ranked 153 out of 187 countries in the 2013 United Nations Development Program Human Development Index. Under-five mortality is estimated at 157 per 1000 live births and maternal mortality is estimated at 545 per 100,000 live births, according to the Demographic and Health Survey (DHS) 2008. For nearly all socioeconomic indicators, the south of the country is significantly better off than the north. For example, under-five mortality rates are about one and a half times higher and maternal mortality rates are three times higher in some northern zones as in the rest of the country. The south west zone has the lowest under-five mortality. The country's gross domestic product has increased during the past decade, with oil revenues as the main driver of the economy. In spite of a high income from crude oil sales, the economic growth has not improved the welfare of the majority of the population or the high incidence of poverty.

Malaria is transmitted throughout Nigeria, with 97% of the population at risk. Five ecological zones define the intensity and seasonality of transmission and mosquito vector species: mangrove swamps; rain forest; Guinea-savannah; Sudan-savannah; and Sahel-savannah. The duration of the transmission season decreases from year-round transmission in the south to three months or less in the north. *Plasmodium falciparum* is the predominant malaria species. The

13

major vectors are *Anopheles (An.) gambiae s. l.* and *An. funestus.* Within the *An. gambiae* complex, *An. arabiensis* predominates in the north and *An. melas* in the mangrove coastal zones.

According to the NMCP Strategic Plan 2009-2013, malaria accounts for about 60% of outpatient visits and 30% of hospitalizations in Nigeria. It is a leading cause of mortality in children under five and is responsible for an estimated 225,000 deaths annually. It also contributes to an estimated 11% of maternal mortality and 10% of low birth weight. Results from the Malaria Indicator Survey (MIS) 2010 showed that more than half of patients with fever first seek treatment in the private sector. Overall, 26% of household members with fever first sought treatment at a government facility. This varied by geopolitical zone (highest in the northwest at 42% and the lowest in the southeast at 7%); by age (highest for children under five at 32%); by residence (urban 22% and rural 27%); and by wealth quintile (lowest quintile 30% and highest quintile 20%).

3. Country health system delivery structure and Ministry of Health organization

The public health care system is divided into three tiers, each associated with one of the administrative levels of government: federal, state, and LGA. While the 774 LGAs are the constitutionally-designated providers of primary health care, they are the weakest arm of the health system. There are more than 13,000 primary health care facilities nationwide. In addition to the federal Ministry of Health (MOH), the National Primary Health Care Development Agency, a centrally-funded agency, has the mandate to support the promotion and implementation of high-quality and sustainable primary health care. This agency is particularly active in development of community-based systems and functional infrastructure as well as ensuring that infants are fully immunized against vaccine-preventable diseases.

The federal budget covers tertiary care and disease control programs, including malaria control; state budgets pay for secondary care; and LGA budgets cover primary care. The amount of government spending on health and malaria is difficult to determine, as funding levels vary and actual spending does not always match the original budget. Health accounts have not yet been established, but it is believed that the government spends less than 5% of the national budget on health.

The public health system in Nigeria is weak. Problems include:

- Poor service delivery at the periphery where most primary health care facilities offer only a limited package of services
- Weak referral linkages between the different levels of health care
- Weak logistics systems for commodities with as many as six separate vertical commodities management systems with little or no coordination between them

14

- Poor health infrastructure with many buildings and equipment in need of repair and/or maintenance
- Weak institutional capacity with inadequate supervision of health services

Led by a coordinator, the NMCP comprises six branches – Program Management, Procurement and Supply Management, Integrated Vector Management, Case Management, Monitoring and Evaluation, and Advocacy, Communication and Social Mobilization (ACSM) – with a total of about 80 staff members. At the national level, the NMCP is responsible for establishing policies, guidelines, and norms. Each state and LGA has a RBM malaria officer (local civil service) who oversees malaria activities in his or her area.

The private health care system is robust and provides care for a substantial proportion of the Nigerian population. It consists of tertiary, secondary, and primary health care facilities, as well as patent medicine vendors (PMVs) and drug sellers. More than 70% of all secondary facilities and about 35% of primary health care facilities in Nigeria are private, and 63% of all fever cases seek treatment first in the private sector (MIS 2010). Services provided by the private sector may be subsidized, as in missionary health facilities, or full-cost, as in privately owned clinics and hospitals. The latter are more common in urban than in rural areas. In rural areas, about two-thirds of the population lives within five kilometers of a primary health care clinic. The estimated 36,000 PMVs nationwide are fairly evenly distributed between urban and rural areas.

4. National malaria control strategy

The NMCP Strategic Plan 2009-2013 is based on the National Strategic Health Development Plan 2010-2015 and is in line with national health and development priorities. The strategy outlines the provision of a comprehensive package of integrated malaria prevention and treatment through the community, primary, secondary, and tertiary levels. The strategy also defines the roles of each health care worker relative to malaria case management and control across all health care services including public, private (including for-profit and not-for-profit), and traditional health providers.

The overall objectives of the NMCP Strategic Plan for the period 2009-2013 are to:

- Provide rapid, national scale-up of a package of high-impact interventions that include appropriate measures to promote positive behavior change, prevention and treatment of malaria; and
- Sustain and consolidate gains through a strengthened health system that establishes the basis for the future elimination of malaria in the country.

This plan has a goal of reducing malaria-related mortality in Nigeria by 50% by the end of 2013. This will be accomplished by reaching the following coverage targets by 2013:

- At least 80% of households have two or more ITNs;
- At least 80% of pregnant women and children under five sleep under an ITN;
- Twenty percent of households nationwide are covered by IRS as a complementary strategy to ITNs, and where conducted, at least 85% of targeted structures are adequately sprayed;
- At least 80% of pregnant women receive two doses of IPTp; and
- At least 80% of patients with fever attending a health facility receive an appropriate malaria diagnostic test, and those testing positive are effectively treated according to the national treatment guidelines.

The federal government supports the provision (free-of-charge) of long-lasting insecticide-treated nets (ITNs), IPTp, IRS, and diagnosis and treatment of uncomplicated and severe malaria. Further description of the strategies is found in the PMI MOP for FY 2013 and in individual intervention sections of this MOP.

5. Integration, collaboration, and coordination

Key International Partners

Nigeria has benefited from increasing support from various partners for malaria control. Currently, the largest partners in terms of funding are the Global Fund, PMI, the World Bank, and the DfID. Other key partners include the Clinton Health Access Initiative, the United Nations Children's Fund (UNICEF), and the World Health Organization (WHO).

The Global Fund Round 8 malaria grant funds the scale-up of prevention and case management activities in line with the NMCP Strategic Plan 2009-2013. The key interventions under this grant are to contribute to universal coverage of ITNs through mass campaigns and routine distribution; to increase ACT rollout in the public and private sectors; and to increase malaria diagnosis using microscopy at referral centers and rollout of rapid diagnostic tests (RDTs) at primary health facilities. In 2010, the Affordable Medicines Facility for malaria (AMFm) was added to help achieve universal access to high-quality, affordable ACTs in all sectors more rapidly. Phase II of the grant, which started in August 2012, has a total budget of $150 million. Combined with the last six months of funds in the Phase I grant, the total budget for the full three-year period of Phase II, from 1 November 2011 until 31 October 2014, is $225 million. Of the $225 million Phase II funds, a $50 million match has been set aside for additional ITNs. These funds will be accessible through an innovative co-financing agreement between the Global Fund and the Nigerian government. For every $1 the Nigerian government contributes for ITNs, the Global Fund will match with $5, up to a total of $50 million.

In Global Fund Round 8 Phase II, approximately seven million ITNs will be purchased for routine distribution in addition to 50 million ACT treatments and 16.5 million RDTs. These commodities will be split between the public and private sectors. The grant will also support information, education, and communication/behavior change communication (BCC); fiduciary management strengthening; Logistical Management Information System (LMIS) strengthening; monitoring and evaluation (M&E) strengthening; training on integrated management of malaria for health workers; revitalization of home-based management of fever; BCC on case management; and pharmacovigilance.

In February 2013, the Global Fund named the Nigeria malaria program as an "interim applicant" during the Global Fund's transition to its new funding model. As such, Nigeria will receive an additional $167 million during the 2013-2014 period. The bulk of this funding – $125 million – will be used to purchase ITNs to replace the 30 million nets distributed in 2009-2011. The remaining $42 million will be used to purchase RDTs and ACTs.

The AMFm pilot provided subsidized ACTs to the private sector. During the pilot, the AMFm provided a 95% subsidy on the price of ACTs and supported the cost of shipping and importation. In 2012, about 65 million treatments were imported under AMFm. Although retail prices dropped substantially (to a median of about 200 naira or $1.26 per treatment), they did not reach the AMFm targets. In November 2012, the Global Fund Board voted to "transition" the AMFm to "full integration" within the Global Fund business model, which means any future funding for subsidies for the private sector will come from the country's Global Fund grant. The The AMFm pilot will transition to full integration in 2013. Nigeria will receive approximately $40 million during the transition, with subsidy levels reduced to 85% for adult doses. The government and partners are exploring alternatives to the AMFm model of drug subsidy as a future strategy for case management in the private sector.

The World Bank Booster Program provided a total of about $280 million in loans between 2007 and 2009 to support seven Nigerian states and central level malaria activities, including ITN campaigns in target states, IRS, and purchases of ACTs, RDTs, and sulfadoxine-pyrimethamine (SP) for malaria control. The project supported training, supervision, and monitoring activites, including two rounds of lot quality assurance sampling surveys, to assess the impact of the program. The Booster Program ended in June 2013, but the country has requested a no cost extension of the project to June 2014. Beyond June 2014, the World Bank may continue to fund malaria activities through its normal lending channels (i.e., the International Development Association).

DfID supports a five-year, £50 million project (about $80 million) called Support for the National Malaria Program (SuNMaP), which started in 2009. Currently, the program is in a period of no cost extension, but DfID has indicated a willingness to maintain funding at similar levels for 2014 and 2015 (£8-10 million per year; with an additional £9-10 million per year for commodities). The program provides substantial support for the NMCP and ten selected states.

In these states, SuNMaP supports malaria prevention, diagnosis, and treatment, and supplies limited quantities of malaria commodities. The SuNMAP also is developing a private sector component that will examine diagnosis and treatment in the private sector, as well as a "market sector" component that will explore market interventions.

The WHO supports a national malaria program officer in each of the six geopolitical zones of Nigeria who assist the states in their zones with malaria program planning and management. The WHO supported the first-ever malaria program review in Nigeria in 2012. The review recommended some strategic shifts for Nigeria, such as using different strategies for different states. All PMI activities are coordinated with these efforts.

The Clinton Health Access Initiative worked closely with the NMCP in the preparation for and management of the AMFm program, particularly in terms of relations with private sector manufacturers and distributors. They have also taken a special interest in promoting the use of injectable artesunate as the first-line treatment for severe malaria. National policy has been changed to reflect the new WHO guidelines and hospitals are being encouraged to purchase this drug.

Private Sector

Although PMI recognizes the potential for private sector approaches in malaria control, the opportunities to work with these organizations under PMI have been limited. Large oil firms carry out their own malaria control activities in their work areas. Some firms also include malaria control in their corporate social responsibility work. Exxon has funded Jhpiego to carry out a study of extending IPTp and other malaria interventions to community-directed distributors in Akwa Ibom State. This study demonstrated the potential of using community-directed distributors and has helped inform PMI plans for ITN upkeep and other activities.

The AMFm program, managed by the Global Fund, has worked with a large number of private importers as "first-line buyers" of subsidized ACTs. Since the AMFm grant was signed in September 2010 and until October 2012, Nigeria had AMFm orders approved for 118.2 million treatments (96.8 million private for-profit, 11.7 million public, and 9.7 million private not-for-profits) of which 98.2 million have been delivered. Most of this has passed through purely private sector channels and has dramatically increased the supply of ACTs in the Nigerian market.

The Private Sector Alliance for MDGs includes polio and malaria as target areas for attention. This alliance is co-chaired by the state minister for health and the former chief executive officer of a Nigerian bank, and the secretariat is supported by Aliku Dangote, one of Nigeria's most prominent businessmen. The NMCP created a committee to seek private sector support and invited Mr. Dangote to be a malaria ambassador for Nigeria. What role the private sector will play through these actions remains unclear. There has been discussion of local production of ITNs and ACTs, but it is unlikely that they could be competitively priced.

18

Within USG

PMI Nigeria has identified opportunities to integrate its work with other activities within the USAID Health Population and Nutrition team, and with other USAID, U.S. Department of Defense (DOD), and President's Emergency Plan for AIDS Relief (PEPFAR) activities. The overarching strategic document for this integration, the United States Global Health Initiative Strategy Document, was completed in September 2011 and took into account the expanding PMI program in Nigeria. In mid-2013, PMI and PEPFAR agreed to collaborate in two states and are considering opportunities to expand collaboration to other states.

Malaria is fully integrated into primary health care supported under the bilateral Targeted State High Impact Project (TSHIP) project, which is active in two of Nigeria's 36 states. In those states all PMI-supported public sector malaria work is channeled through this project.

Malaria was included in the Expanded Social Marketing Program in Nigeria. This collaboration leverages this project's large presence in terms of mass media BCC (national radio drama, spots/jingles, and a weekly radio magazine), and interpersonal approaches (community-based interpersonal communication in 15 priority states). Malaria messaging is included at low cost. This program also provides a link through mobile drug suppliers to drug vendors and private sector providers since the lead on this project, the Society for Family Health (SFH), is also a Principal Recipient of the Global Fund Round 8 malaria grant. Mobile suppliers working with SFH also efficiently combine malaria, family planning and maternal/child health messages with product promotion. Malaria funds also leverage the large reach of the Voice of America Hausa language service in northern Nigeria.

Support for improved diagnostics has built on the base provided by the PEPFAR DOD-Walter Reed Program to improve HIV-related laboratory services. This program included improved malaria microscopy and RDT use under PEPFAR as management of an opportunistic infection. PMI is expanding on this base to support malaria activities.

PMI and PEPFAR are working to support Nigeria's integrated Health Management Information System (HMIS). This is requiring a shift from the NMCP's previous parallel system, which was created to support Global Fund reporting, and from the parallel PEPFAR HIV system. It will take some time for the new system to become operational, but it is already active in several states and should eventually replace the older systems.

Steps are being taken to integrate approaches to logistics support for PEPFAR, PMI, and USAID-supported family planning programs. This is particularly promising in terms of warehousing, which is a challenge in Nigeria. In Ebonyi State, family planning and malaria funds are jointly supporting an innovative model – Direct Delivery and Information Capture – to improve distribution within states and collect better facility-level consumption data.

PMI is cooperating more intensively with the PEPFAR program in two states, Benue and Cross River, which have a PMI presence and are a PEPFAR priority because of the relatively high HIV prevalence. This cooperation includes shared warehousing, PEPFAR-procured ITNs, ACTs, and RDTs, and laboratory strengthening activities in the form of combined training, supervision, and quality assurance of laboratories for malaria, HIV, and tuberculosis testing. This cooperation will expand malaria prevention and treatment programs in these two states, providing better protection of target populations.

6. PMI goals, targets, and indicators

The goal of PMI is to reduce malaria-associated mortality by 50% in new countries added to the PMI in FY 2010 and later. By the end of 2014, PMI will assist Nigeria to achieve the following targets in populations at risk for malaria:

- >90% of households with a pregnant woman and/or children under five will own at least one ITN;
- 85% of children under five will have slept under an ITN the previous night;
- 85% of pregnant women will have slept under an ITN the previous night;
- 85% of houses in geographic areas targeted for IRS will have been sprayed
- 85% of pregnant women and children under five will have slept under an ITN the previous night or in a house that has been sprayed with IRS in the last 6 months;
- 85% of women who have completed a pregnancy in the last two years will have received two or more doses of IPTp during that pregnancy; and
- 85% of government health facilities have ACTs available for treatment of uncomplicated malaria.

7. Progress on coverage/impact indicators to date

The most up-to-date official information on the status of malaria control efforts in Nigeria is the Nigeria MIS 2010 (December) and the MICS 2011 (March). A National HIV/AIDS and Reproductive Health Survey from 2012 included an ITN module, but results are pending. Data collection for the DHS 2013 has begun and includes a malaria module.

Selected national-level results from the MIS 2010 are shown in Table A. Malaria prevalence based on microscopy indicated that 42% of children aged 6-59 months had malaria parasites. Parasitemia was higher in rural areas (48%) than in urban areas (22%) and decreased as a mother's education level improved. Variation in indicators by geopolitical zone was reported (Figure 3). The highest malaria prevalence zones were South West (50%), North Central (49%), and North West (48%), while the lowest prevalence zones were South East (28%), North East (31%), and South South (32%).

Figure 3: Map of malaria prevalence by geopolitical region in Nigeria, 2010

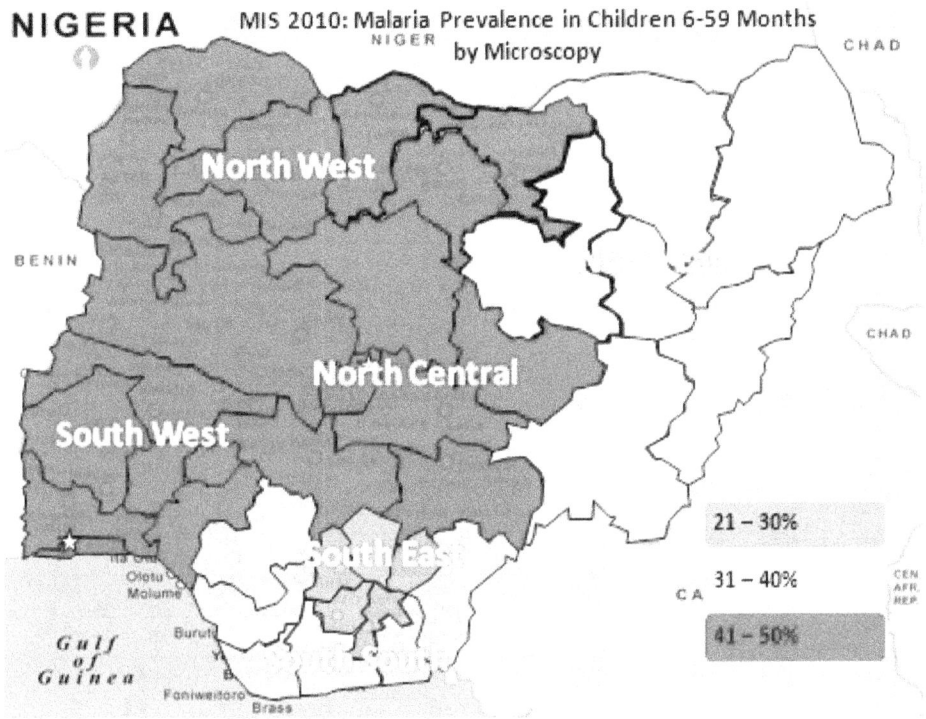

Insecticide-treated net ownership increased from 8% in DHS 2008 to 42% in MIS 2010. The MICS 2011 survey reported overall ITN ownership at 40%. Both the MIS 2010 and MICS 2011 showed differences in the coverage rates by geopolitical zone. The MICS 2011 reported lower levels of ITN utilization by children under five and pregnant women in all zones except South West, with markedly lower utilization rates in the three northern zones. The largest decrease in reported ITN use between the MIS 2010 and MICS 2011 occurred in the North East: rates among children under five went from 74% to 24%, while pregnant women dropped from 75% to 30%. Seasonal differences likely account for the lower utilization, as the MICS 2011 survey was conducted during the dry season and the MIS 2010 during the rainy season.

Table A: Reported ITN Ownership and Use from MIS 2010 and MICS 2011 by Geopolitical Zone

Geopolitical Zone	Survey	Percentage of households with at least one ITN (%)	Percentage of children under five years old who slept under an ITN the previous night in a household with an ITN (%)	Percentage of pregnant women who slept under an ITN the previous night in a household with an ITN (%)
North Central	MIS 2010	32.1	49.5	70.3
	MICS 2011	38.1	28.8	40.7
North East	MIS 2010	62.9	73.5	74.9
	MICS 2011	51.2	24.2	29.5
North West	MIS 2010	58.2	63.3	73.5
	MICS 2011	62.5	33.9	34.2
South East	MIS 2010	32.2	42.0	29.6
	MICS 2011	31.2	26.8	23.5
South South	MIS 2010	43.8	55.1	48.1
	MICS 2011	41.9	41.9	39.3
South West	MIS 2010	20.3	28.8	49.0
	MICS2011	20.7	39.2	42.6

Under-five ITN utilization in 2010 was 29% overall and was 59% in those households that owned an ITN; however, the MICS 2011 reported 16% overall use and 33% in households that owned at least one ITN. The MIS 2010 reported that nationally, 34% of pregnant women slept under an ITN the previous night and in households with an ITN, the percentage was 66%. The MICS 2011 reported 17% overall use by pregnant women and 35% in households that owned at least one ITN. These results indicate that access to and ownership of ITNs are the priorities for reaching universal coverage.

The proportion of women who received two or more doses of SP during their last pregnancy has remained low with 5% in DHS 2008, 13% in MIS 2010, and 20% in MICS 2011.

The MIS 2010 reports that, of children under five with fever, only about 49% received any antimalarial treatment, while the MICS 2011 reports 45%. Of those children who received malaria treatment, the MIS 2010 indicates 12% took an ACT, while 10% took an ACT in the MICS 2011. In contrast, those who took chloroquine or SP were 79% (MIS 2010) and 64% (MICS 2011). The MIS 2010 reported that 5% of children under five with fever had a blood test taken, while the MICS 2011 showed 8%.

A sub-analysis of the MIS that aggregated the data from PMI focus states has been completed. These results are also included in Table B and act as a baseline. Note that at the end of 2010, all of the ITN indicators were worse in the PMI focus states than for national level. This is due to a larger proportion of PMI focus states not having completed ITN universal campaigns as compared with the national coverage. Results for PMI show that ITN ownership of at least one net was only 30%; under-five ITN use was 21%, and malaria prevalence among children under five by microscopy stood at 47%.

Table B. Malaria Indicators, Nigeria, 2008-2010

	Est. National Coverage (2008 DHS)	Est. National Coverage (2010 MIS)	PMI-Focus States (2010 MIS)
Proportion of households with at least one ITN	8.0%	41.5%	30.0%
Proportion of children under five years old who slept under an ITN the previous night	5.5%	29.1%	20.7%
Proportion of children under five years old who slept under an ITN the previous night in a household with an ITN	49.8%	59.0%	51.2%
Proportion of pregnant women who slept under an ITN the previous night	4.8%	33.7%	20.0%
Proportion of pregnant women who slept under an ITN the previous night in a household with an ITN	44.4%	65.6%	48.4%
Proportion of children under five years old with fever in the last two weeks who received treatment with ACTs within 24 hours	1.1%	3.2%	2.5%
Proportion of children under five years old with fever in the last two weeks given any antimalarial within 24 hours that received an ACT	7.0%	12.0%	16.0%
Proportion of women who received an antimalarial drug during their last pregnancy leading to a live birth within the previous two years	18.4%	29.6%	23.3%
Proportion of women who received two or more doses of IPTp during their last pregnancy leading to a live birth within the previous two years (IPTp)	4.9%*	13.2%*	9.7%*
Percentage of children aged 6-59 months with malaria infection detected by microscopy	n/a	42.0	47.2
Percentage of children aged 6-59 months with hemoglobin lower than 8.0 g/dL	n/a	12.6	9.7
*during an antenatal visit			

23

There are often challenges and opportunities for multiple aspects of malaria control and will be presented as such below.

Commodity procurement and supply management

Challenges: The commodity supply system remains a huge challenge in Nigeria. The system is multifaceted, and at the federal level is built around the needs for specific projects and diseases. It remains a challenge given the multiple procurers, variable supply chains between and within states, lack of reliable consumption data from all levels in the reporting system, and generally weak logistics management systems. These factors make it difficult to establish a management system to track supply and develop a rational forecasting, ordering, and distribution system for malaria commodities.

Opportunities: Working at state level, PMI has the opportunity to develop new innovative approaches that can be expanded nationally. In addition, improved communication and collaboration between PMI and Global Fund at the national level opens up new opportunities for better coordination and pooled distribution of malaria commodities at the state level. Finally, PMI is expanding on collaboration with PEPFAR in two states, Benue and Cross River, that have potential for a unified distribution system.

Private sector delivery of malaria prevention and treatment

Challenges: Many Nigerians, including those under five, first seek care for fevers from the private sector (MIS 2010). While most PMVs have received some informal training to recognize uncomplicated malaria, they are not empowered to diagnose the disease. Also, many are not aware of NMCP guidelines for malaria treatment. These issues, along with the price of ACTs being higher than many patients can afford, lead to patients not receiving optimal case management in this sector.

Opportunities: PMI has supported pilot interventions to improve parasitological diagnosis in the private sector. Depending on the results of the pilots, the PMI will consider increasing support for scaling up interventions.

Larviciding

Challenges: Government investment in larviciding is a substantial challenge for Nigeria. The government recently took out a $270 million loan to build a bio-larviciding factory in Rivers state. Political commitment to the project comes from the highest levels of government. At the same time, there is a misperception among some in high levels of government that bed nets do not work and are not a good intervention for malaria control. The WHO recently issued an interim position statement on larviciding that discusses pros and cons of this costly, labor- and equipment-intensive intervention. The WHO discourages the use of larviciding except in special situations that meet certain criteria.

Opportunities: PMI needs to work with RBM partners to provide further evidence that nets are working in Nigeria and demonstrate that high coverage needs to be maintained. Another opportunity for PMI is to join WHO and other partners to continue advocating for a solid evidence base to inform any large-scale implementation of larviciding.

Insecurity and civil unrest

Challenges: Violent attacks, particularly in the north of the country, threaten the government and various government- and donor-funded programs. Travel restrictions were put in place in 2012, limiting movement of USG staff in certain parts of the country. All travel requires advance approval from the embassy Regional Security Office and all travel outside Abuja must be in a fully armored vehicle.

9. PMI support strategy

Three important factors influence PMI's support strategy. A key factor is Nigeria's size and the burden of malaria in the country. Nigeria is by far the most populous country in Africa (with an estimated 2014 population of 172 million), and almost the entire country suffers from high levels of endemic malaria. PMI focuses on 11 states with a population of about 50 million, or about 30% of the total Nigerian population. Second, the government in Nigeria is highly decentralized. About half of Nigeria's government revenues go directly to the 36 states and the Federal Capitol Territory of Abuja, as well as the 774 local governments. The federal level has relatively little influence over how these funds are used or whether states have to follow national policies. The federal level is mostly responsible for referral hospitals, while primary health care, including malaria, is more a state and local responsibility. Public health systems expend a great deal of their funds on staffing, but support for commodities tends to be very low and uneven. State-level management of programs, such as malaria control, tends to be very weak. Third, significant support from other donors, such as the Global Fund, World Bank, and DfID, combined with decentralized governance, has led the NMCP and the GoN to pair donors with specific states across the country.

Within this context, PMI's strategy is to work with the national level on policy, forecasting, and state support activities, while selecting specific states, in collaboration with the NMCP, to receive more intensive support for a broad range of malaria control activities. States are chosen to avoid overlap, as much as possible, with the large World Bank- and DfID-supported programs. For activities planned with FY 2014 funds, PMI intends to continue to support the same 11 states. In each state, project teams support the State Malaria Control Program (SMCP) office and assist with planning and implementation of preventive, diagnostic, and treatment programs. Even in the 11 states, PMI is not able to support all commodity needs and is lobbying both the states and national government to take on a larger role in purchasing malaria-related commodities.

The rollout of diagnosis and treatment in the seven Malaria Action Programs for State (MAPS) target states in the first year was limited to the local government hospital and three of the larger primary health care units in each LGA. This was done to gain experience with setting up the logistics system, to learn whether practitioners actually use and follow RDT/microscopy results, and to see whether utilization increases rapidly when facilities' stocks and services are provided for very low prices. Starting with a limited set of facilities allowed lessons learned to guide expansion and protect against PMI stockouts of ACTs and RDTs. Given the early results, the project is expanding to cover four additional public primary health units for a total of eight facilities per LGA, reaching approximately 50% coverage of facilities and an estimated 70% of those seeking treatment at public health facilities.

During its existence, the large AMFm program supported -and the Global Fund continues to support- increased availability and use of ACTs. PMI has therefore limited its work in this area to supporting generic communications and using FY 2012 funds to provide technical assistance for drug quality control. PMI is working with partners to determine alternative ways to support diagnosis and treatment in the private sector.

PMI identifies areas of comparative advantage among partners and focuses support to the most appropriate interventions. For example PMI supports malaria logistics systems and provides technical assistance to national mass ITN distribution campaigns. PMI has chosen to limit IRS activities in Nigeria to two local governments that have protected a population of about 300,000 in the previous two years. This was done to demonstrate high quality IRS training and implementation from which others could learn. It was based on the observation that a number of states in Nigeria are willing to fund IRS themselves but do not have access to strong technical assistance. In FY 2014, PMI will redirect its support from IRS to vector surveillance and susceptibility monitoring in six geopolitical zones around Nigeria.

III. OPERATIONAL PLAN

PREVENTION

1. Insecticide-treated nets (ITNs)

NMCP and PMI Objectives

The NMCP Strategic Plan 2009-2013 sets universal coverage of all population groups as its goal, defined in 2011 as one ITN for every two persons and using the WHO-recommended 1 ITN for every 1.8 persons ratio for quantification. The GoN strategy calls for reaching 80% of all households owning two or more long-lasting ITNs by 2010, and sustaining this coverage through 2013. The strategy sets a target of ensuring that at least 80% of children under five and pregnant women consistently sleep under an ITN. It calls for an initial phase of rapid scale-up of free ITNs through mass distribution campaigns followed by a second phase of replacing torn or worn-out nets through routine services, free or subsidized distribution from community-based organizations and similar structures, and subsidized or full-cost nets distributed through the commercial sector. Schools are not specifically mentioned but the NMCP is supportive to operations research on using school-based delivery channels.

Insecticide treated net ownership increased from 8% in DHS 2008 to 42% in MIS 2010. The MICS 2011 survey reported overall ITN ownership at 40%. Both the MIS 2010 and MICS 2011 showed differences in the coverage rates by geopolitical zone. More detailed information on the coverage and use of ITNs in Nigeria is presented in the "Progress on coverage/impact indicators" section above. Although there are obvious indications of improvement, the Nigeria MIS 2010 documented the challenges of attaining high ITN ownership and use despite efforts by the NMCP and its partners.

PMI's goal is to support the NMCP in achieving and maintaining its coverage and use targets, with a particular emphasis on the 11 PMI focus states. To do this PMI and partners will use a mix of distribution approaches. All 27 states that conducted universal coverage campaigns before 2012 will require a second universal campaign to again achieve high coverage. For the nine states with campaigns held in 2012 and 2013, including two PMI focus states, a vigorous effort to push nets through various continuous distribution channels is needed to keep coverage high. PMI is taking the following steps to increase continuous delivery:

- Strengthen the delivery of ITNs through health facility routine antenatal and vaccination clinics; and
- Explore additional distribution channels and scale up those with strong evidence of success at reasonable cost.

Social marketing has been used successfully in some areas of Nigeria in the past and the SFH continues this approach at a modest level with Global Fund procured ITNs. In addition, there is a vibrant ITN private sector, particularly in the North of the country and partners are investigating ways to increase social marketing and commercial sector sales of ITNs.

Progress during the past 12 months

PMI Nigeria procured about 5.2 million ITNs between January 2012 and March 2013, and provided logistic and BCC support to universal coverage campaigns in Kogi and Oyo states, the first universal coverage campaigns in these states and the last to use the former national target of two ITNs per household (as opposed to the new target of one ITN per two people). With PMI support and with co-funding from the Global Fund, Sokoto will conduct its second universal coverage campaign in 2013. Two million of the 5.2 million ITNs went to support continuous distribution approaches in the other focus states, principally through antenatal care (ANC) and Expanded Program for Immunization (EPI) clinics.

In March 2013 Global Fund announced that Nigeria would receive an additional $167 million of interim funding and plans have been made to procure over 25 million ITNs for delivery in 2014. The World Bank plans to procure 10.1 million and PMI an additional 6.3 million ITNs for delivery in 2014. Building on donor partnerships, PMI will co-fund universal coverage campaigns with the Global Fund in Kebbi, one of the new PMI-focus states, and with the World Bank in Bauchi. PMI will also support a universal coverage campaign in 2014 in Nasarawa and provide 2.2 million ITNs to other PMI focus states for continuous distribution.

PMI is supporting critical operations research activities in three states to investigate key issues that are highly relevant for Nigeria and more broadly for the malaria community. First, PMI is investigating the durability of different brands of ITNs in three different ecological and cultural settings in Nigeria. Second, PMI Nigeria is evaluating new continuous distribution channels, including school-based and community-based distribution approaches to sustain high, equitable coverage between campaigns. Baseline surveys have been completed for these studies and preliminary results are expected for the school-based distribution in early 2014 and for the community-based approaches in late 2014/early 2015. Third, PMI is investigating methods for determining to what extent appropriate care and repair can prolong the useful the life an ITN at the household level. A baseline and one follow-up survey have been completed. Preliminary results are expected in early 2014.

A PMI and PEPFAR collaboration began in 2013 with the goal of ensuring that all pregnant women living in selected states with high malaria prevalence and high numbers of HIV cases receive an ITN as part of their ANC clinic visits. PEPFAR will procure and deliver costs for a total of 550,000 ITNs, 300,000 for in Benue State and 250,000 for Cross River State.

Challenges, opportunities, and threats

Opportunities: The $167 million of Global Fund Interim Funding for Nigeria's malaria programs, earmarked to support the second mass ITN campaign in states that completed their first statewide mass campaigns before 2012, creates significant opportunities for collaboration to achieve Nigeria's goals.

Challenges: Some studies indicate that the attrition and rate of deterioration of ITNs in Nigeria is high.[1] PMI is promoting care and repair to extend the life of nets and will work with partners to improve net use in areas where surveys have indicated it is low.

Commodity gap analysis

The projected need for continuous distribution in PMI focus states is presented in Table C below.

Table C: Gap analysis for universal coverage campaigns and continuous distribution at ANC and EPI clinics

States[1]	2013 Popula-tion	2013 need	2013 input	2014 need[1]	2014 input	2015 need[1]	2015 input
Universal coverage campaign (in millions)							
Bauchi	5.9	3.26		3.36	3.27		
Benue	5.1					2.96	
Cross River	3.4			2.00		2.02	2.02
Ebonyi	2.6					1.52	
Kogi	3.9					2.36	
Nasarawa	2.3			1.28	1.28		
Oyo	6.6	3.67	2.75				
Sokoto	4.4	2.44	2.44				
Zamfara	3.9			2.22		2.29	2.29

---

1 Toju Maleghemi S, Erskine M: CROSS RIVER Qualitative survey to account for missing nets; Alliance for Malaria Prevention Annual Meeting, February 2011.

Total (PMI input)	38.1	9.37	5.19 (3.00)	8.86	4.55 (3.01)	11.15	4.31 (4.31)
Gap			4.18		4.31		6.84
Continuous distribution through ANC and EPI							
Bauchi	5.9	0.246	0.271	0.252	0.277	0.258	0.258
Benue	5.1	0.213	0.234	0.218	0.24	0.223	0.223
Cross River	3.4	0.142	0.156	0.145	0.160	0.149	0.149
Ebonyi	2.6	0.108	0.119	0.111	0.122	0.114	0.114
Kogi	3.9	0.163	0.179	0.167	0.183	0.171	0.171
Nasarawa	2.3	0.096	0.105	0.098	0.108	0.101	0.101
Oyo	6.6	0.275	0.303	0.282	0.310	0.289	0.289
Sokoto	4.4	0.183	0.202	0.188	0.207	0.193	0.193
Zamfara	3.9	0.163	0.150	0.167	0.183	0.171	0.171
Total need (PMI input)[3]	38.1	1.588	1.718 (1.718)	1.628	1.790 (1.790)	1.668	1.668 (.800)
Gap (surplus)			(.310)		(.162)		.868

NOTE: Shaded boxes under the Universal Coverage Campaign section indicate that a campaign occurred in the past three years and no campaign is needed yet.

1. The table reflects commodity gaps in the nine original states; the two new states were added too late in the FY 2014 operational planning cycle to be included in the FY 2014 budget; these states will be included reprogramming of additional FY 2013 funding and potential new appropriations in FY 2014.
2. The 2014 and 2015 need for universal campaigns takes into account yearly population increases of 2.5% from the 2013 base
3. Need for continuous distribution through ANC and EPI is calculated using an annual birth rate of 40/1000 for all states; ANC and EPI attendance for the geopolitical region taken from the 2011 MICS were then used to calculate state needs

Plans and Justification

Five PMI focus states will require universal coverage campaigns in 2015: Benue, Cross River, Ebonyi, Kogi and Zamfara. At the present funding level, two of the five states can be fully covered (Zamfara and Cross River) and have been identified for universal coverage campaigns. PMI is committed to providing support for continuous distribution and will supply all states with an adequate supply of ITNs to very nearly cover the needs for ANC and EPI distribution. If additional funds are available, PMI will support other continuous distribution approaches, such as school-based distribution, provided that ongoing studies show these to be effective approaches. Other partners, particularly Global Fund, may help fill the gap in PMI focus states, but no commitment has been made for 2015.

PMI Nigeria will invest in scaling up ITN care and repair across PMI states if ongoing studies in Nasarawa indicate that these interventions are effective in prolonging the useful life of ITNs.

Description and budget for proposed activities with FY 2014 funding ($25,927,000):

1. *Procure approximately 5.1 million ITNs* that will be used to support mass campaigns in Zamfara and Cross River (4.3 million ITNs) and continuous distribution in all PMI focus states (.8 million). ($20,977,000)

2. *Logistic and operational support for distribution of ITNs* for the three mass campaigns and for sustaining gains following mass campaigns in PMI focus states. Support for continuous distribution will include delivery through routine services, as well as innovative approaches to reach vulnerable populations and to maintain high population coverage. This also includes the development of systems for regular distribution, storage, supervision, and reporting in each of nine PMI focus states. ($4,650,000)

3. *Technical assistance* to support the scaling up of evidence-based continuous ITN distribution and net care and repair approaches to all PMI focus states, as appropriate. If the findings from operations research activities in Nigeria and Uganda demonstrate that care and repair of ITNs can prolong the viable life of an ITN, PMI will disseminate and implement the best practices directly through implementing partners and through the NMCP to other in-country partners. If the results from those studies do not have positive outcomes, PMI will reprogram these funds. ($300,000)

4. *Support for BCC for malaria prevention and treatment.* Four PMI implementing partners are engaged in BCC activities, including interpersonal communication (IPC), mass media and social mobilization to promote ITN ownership and use, as well as other key aspects of malaria control and prevention. (Costs covered under the ACSM section)

NMCP and PMI Objectives

Nigeria's NMCP Strategic Plan 2009-2013 calls for vector control as part of an integrated vector management strategy and includes universal access to ITNs; increased IRS in targeted areas where ITNs alone are not impacting malaria transmission; environmental management to reduce available mosquito breeding sites in urban and peri-urban areas; and larval control using larvicides, predators, or growth inhibitors where this is feasible and sustainable. In 2006-2007, several IRS trials using four pyrethroids and a carbamate (bendiocarb) were conducted in five LGAs, one in each of five states, in collaboration with insecticide manufacturing companies. This was expanded to seven states (Akwa Ibom, Anambra, Bauchi, Gombe, Jigawa, Kano, and Rivers) in 2009 with financial assistance from the World Bank. The WHO vector control staff evaluated these trials and concluded that IRS is feasible and should be scaled up in Nigeria.

According to the NMCP Strategic Plan 2009-2013, spraying would be focused in areas: with a short transmission season where the addition of IRS might make local elimination feasible; where ITN implementation is difficult and use is low; and where IRS may have a greater impact, such as in and around more densely populated municipalities. The objective of this plan was to scale up IRS to cover seven million households by the end of 2013, or 20% nationwide. Support from the Nigerian government at national and/or state level for IRS is essential to meet the stated goals.

Progress during the past 12 months

PMI collaborated with the NMCP and other partners to demonstrate what is required for a well-run IRS program in Nasarawa State. This included technical, strategic, managerial, and operational support to implement IRS in two LGAs, Doma and Nasarawa Eggon. In 2012 and 2013, PMI-supported IRS protected 300,000 people in approximately 65,000 structures in those two LGAs; PMI direct operational support of this program is ending after the 2013 spray season is finished, fulfilling an earlier arrangement with the MOH to provide IRS training and oversight for two years. Continuation of IRS activities in LGAs from which PMI has withdrawn will become the responsibility of state or local government. An ITN universal coverage campaign is planned for 2014 in Nasarawa with PMI funds to protect those people who lose IRS in these two LGAs. PMI stands ready to provide IRS technique training and technical assistance to NMCP if requested.

Activities supported with PMI FY 2012 funding included a supplemental environmental assessment to comply with Nigerian and U.S. environmental regulations, geographical reconnaissance (including basic mapping and enumeration of structures in the spray area), and a logistics assessment to quantify needed commodities. Vector-related activities supported by PMI included testing to establish baseline vector susceptibility to different classes of IRS-approved insecticides (with input from NMCP and WHO), species identification, procurement of insecticide and other IRS commodities, IRS operations in Nasarawa State, and core IRS training of Nigerian public health officers. PMI supported a one-week training session on malaria vector bionomics, identification, surveillance and the CDC bottle bioassay procedure for insecticide resistance detection, assessment, and management. More than 50 people including Vector Control Officers from each of the 36 states and the Federal District attended this training. PMI's major objective will shift with FY 2014 funding from IRS to an NMCP-led national surveillance program for vector bionomics and insecticide resistance monitoring. Advocacy for IRS will be supported, and training will continue as requested with partner organizations, with appropriate government officials at all levels, and with private organizations.

Challenges, opportunities, and threats

As PMI withdraws from direct IRS spray operations, the intent is to transition this intervention to the state and/or local government. Nigerian states will assume responsibility for the IRS programs, with PMI available for technical consultation and assistance, as needed. PMI will continue to work with the NMCP to update the national IRS strategy and will provide training in spray operations and other educational opportunities in 2014 and beyond as requested. The World Bank, in collaboration with insecticide manufacturing companies, RBM, and PMI, were the only donors supporting IRS, but World Bank support of IRS will end in 2013.

Opportunity: Significant in-country funds exist that can support IRS, especially the Nigerian MDG Debt Relief Fund, which has approximately $1 billion in annual funding, part of which has been used to purchase ITNs. The MDG Debt Relief Fund has indicated its willingness to fund IRS if it receives suitable proposals. However, it remains to be seen if MDG Debt Relief Fund will provide funding and how much.

The NMCP is now seeking comprehensive technical and financial support to begin malaria vector surveillance at six sites around the country in line with development of their upcoming NMCP Strategic Plan 2014-2018. PMI will provide technical assistance for planning the program, along with equipment and funding for implementation. These fixed sentinel sites will monitor vector populations for species composition, seasonality, and insecticide resistance. Published resistance data is scattered from around the country and lacks longevity. Light trap captures, pyrethrum spray catches, and indoor/outdoor resting densities of malaria vectors will be conducted six times a year to determine seasonality of vectors in each of the six zones. Although NMCP supports human landing catches as a surveillance tactic, PMI will not support this method due to the risk of infection to collectors.

Threat: Insecticide resistance in malaria vectors to pyrethroid insecticides in increasing across Africa. Limited resistance status data have been collected piecemeal from Nigeria, and recent surveys indicate that resistance is developing in spot locations. PMI conducted resistance testing in Nasarawa Eggon in 2011 and 2012, and complete susceptibility to pyrethroids was seen in 2011. However, in 2012 probable resistance was observed for pyrethroids using both WHO tube and CDC bottle bioassay tests (see Table D for 24hr mortality rates from Oct 2012. For each test at least 100 mosquitoes were used).

Table D: Insecticide Susceptibility Testing results using WHO tube and CDC bottle bioassays on a minimum of 100 female *Anopheles gambiae* s.l., Nasarawa State, Nigeria, 2012.*

Insecticide	Class	WHO tube (24 hr) (% mortality)	CDC bottle (30 min) (% mortality)
Alpha cypermethrin	Pyrethroid	100	89
Deltamethrin	Pyrethroid	88.5	94
Lambda-cyhalothrin	Pyrethroid	84.3	97
Fenitrothion	Organophosphate	100	100
Bendiocarb	Carbamate	100	100

* For WHO test, < 90% mortality = resistance; CDC test <95% mortality = resistance

Resistance testing will occur at each of six geopolitical sites during FY 2014 to determine a baseline of susceptibility or resistance in vectors to DDT, organophosphate, carbamate, and pyrethroid insecticides. Tests will be conducted annually to monitor resistance through time.

Challenge: Nigeria has invested in a larvicide production facility in Rivers State. This plant will produce *Bacillus thuringensis israelinsis*, a mosquito larvicide that kills larvae by a different mode of action from IRS insecticides approved by the WHO Pesticide Evaluation Scheme. Unfortunately, effective larviciding requires frequent applications due to short residual life (< one week), is labor-intensive, costly and requires an extensive equipment infrastructure to be effective. In some situations, larviciding can be useful where breeding sites are fixed, few, and findable[2]. Larviciding is not an intervention recommended by PMI, and PMI's position is that programs that do undertake larviciding should adhere to the WHO Larviciding Interim Position Statement.

Plans and Justification

PMI considers monitoring of insecticide resistance and collection of vector bionomics to be vital to Nigeria. PMI will support the NMCP to establish entomologic surveillance sites in each of the six geopolitical zones that will serve for annual monitoring of malaria vector susceptibility to six WHO-approved IRS compounds from all four insecticide classes. Vector species and indoor and outdoor densities will be monitored at these six sites every other month to determine seasonality

---

1   Malaria – Nigeria. ProMED mail post, 2 May, 2012. http://www.promedmail.org/direct.php?id=20120502.1120714
2   Interim Position Statement, WHO. The role of larviciding for malaria control in sub-Saharan Africa. April 2012, #2.

and vector composition for each site. PMI will assist NMCP in developing an updated National Malaria Integrated Vector Control Strategy if requested.

Description and budget for proposed activities with FY 2014 funding ($1,055,000):

1. *Provide support for vector surveillance and susceptibility monitoring in six geopolitical zones around Nigeria.* Supervision, entomological monitoring, per diem, vehicle rentals and equipment necessary to survey malaria vectors in six geopolitical zones throughout the country to determine vector species, seasonality, parity rates and indoor densities six times a year, and insecticide susceptibility status to four classes of insecticide once a year. ($550,000)

2. *Strengthen capacity for entomological expertise at federal and state levels.* Strengthen capacity for entomological competence at federal and state levels with training and equipment support (WHO cone wall bioassays, light trap collections, pyrethrum spray collections, surveillance equipment training, larval surveillance, insecticide susceptibility training) to perform these activities. Provide IRS technical assistance and training as requested by NMCP. ($450,000)

3. *Technical assistance to PMI IRS activities.* This will include three temporary duty trips to provide insecticide resistance training for Nigerian IRS staff, resistance test kits, and insecticide for Nigerian staff attending training, training in IRS technique, and a review of surveillance activities in six geopolitical zones with implementing partners. ($55,000)

3. Intermittent preventive treatment for pregnant women (IPTp)

NMCP and PMI Objectives

Each year, Nigeria has an estimated seven and a half million pregnant women, almost all of whom are at risk of malaria. The burden of malaria in pregnancy (MIP) is high with significant health and economic impact.

To reduce the negative consequences of MIP – such as low birth weight, preterm deliveries, spontaneous abortions, in-utero growth retardation, and maternal anemia – the Nigeria National Malaria Strategy (2005) called for the scale-up of IPTp with SP; use of ITNs by pregnant women; and prompt, effective treatment of clinical malaria episodes. The current IPTp policy in Nigeria calls for IPTp to be administered as a one-dose preventive treatment course after quickening and the second dose not earlier than one month after the first dose. The two doses are to be taken as a directly observed treatment in ANC clinics. In 2013, WHO issued new policy guidance on IPTp calling for a minimum of three doses, each dose one month apart after the onset of quickening. The doses should be administered at least four weeks apart and given as directly observed therapy. The last dose of SP can be administered safely up to delivery. The NMCP is planning to update its IPTp policy to align with the new guidance. The revised NMCP Strategic Plan 2009-2013 emphasizes that MIP interventions are a component of the focused antenatal care (FANC) services delivered by Reproductive Health/Maternal Child Health Units. USAID/Nigeria's efforts to strengthen collaboration and integration among interventions that impact women and children are consistent with the strategic plan.

Nationally, 60% of pregnant women attend ANC, but utilization varies significantly by region and state. The proportion of women who received two or more doses of SP during their last pregnancy at an antenatal visit was 5% in 2008 (DHS), 13% in 2010 (MIS), and 20% in 2011 (MICS). The key indicator and target for IPTp, listed in the National Malaria Strategic Plan 2009-2013, is for 100% of pregnant women attending ANC services, representing 60% of all pregnant women, to receive at least two doses of IPTp by 2010, and increasing to 80% of all pregnant women by 2013. The latter target will be achieved when ANC clinic utilization rises to 80% and 100% of those women receive at least two doses of IPTp.

Progress on coverage and use of ITN by pregnant women in Nigeria is presented in detail in the "Progress on coverage/impact indicators" section above. In this current national malaria strategic plan, the malaria target is for at least 80% of pregnant women to sleep under an ITN by 2010 and to sustain coverage until 2013.

Progress during the past 12 months

To boost performance of MIP interventions in Nigeria, PMI continued supporting capacity building of service providers to improve delivery of FANC services in the nine PMI focus states. With FY 2012 funding, PMI trained over 1,600 ANC service providers on prevention and management of malaria in pregnancy.

To improve access to critical commodities, PMI procured 3 million treatments of SP, of which 1 million have been delivered and 670,000 distributed to supported states. This quantity is expected to fill the gap in the nine PMI focus states. In 2012, serious delays were experienced in the procurement and delivery of SP to Nigeria. SP cannot be imported into Nigeria without a waiver, and USG regulations do not allow local procurement. However, PMI received a waiver for SP from the National Agency for Food and Drug Administration and Control (NAFDAC), which allowed SP procurement and delivery to proceed in 2013. Some states and local governments are procuring limited amounts of SP, and PMI is advocating for increases in annual budgets for IPTp.

A PMI - PEPFAR collaboration started in 2012 with the goal of ensuring that all pregnant women living in selected states with high malaria prevalence and high numbers of HIV cases receive an ITN as part of their antenatal care clinic visits. In 2013, PEPFAR will procure and cover delivery costs for 550,000 ITNs – 300,000 for Benue and 250,000 for Cross River. During 2013, PMI will procure an additional 2 million ITNs to support continuous distribution approaches in other focus states, principally through ANC and EPI clinics. According to the National Guidelines for Diagnosis and Treatment of Malaria (2011), quinine is safe for treatment of malaria in all trimesters of pregnancy. In the second and third trimester, ACTs can be used. Since quinine is relatively cheap and available, it is included in the Essential Medicines List, which enables the GoN to procure it.

With FY 2012 funding, PMI supported a study on the social, cultural and economic factors that serve as barriers to uptake of IPTp in two states – Cross River and Nasarawa. The study confirmed significant gaps between ANC attendance and uptake of IPTp among pregnant women. It identified social and community factors – such as the support or disapproval of spouses or partners, relatives and friends –that affect women's health-seeking behavior relating to MIP. Uptake of IPTp is also constrained by perceptions of rude and unfriendly attitudes of health workers and system factors, such as long waits and the requirement to pay for prescription drugs. Further, front-line health workers indicated they do not have sufficient training and experience in FANC that integrates malaria prevention and treatment. The study report recommended communication programs to mobilize communities as a whole, rather than seeking to change individual behavior in piecemeal fashion and hoping for "trickle-down" or "trickle-up" effects. PMI is supporting communication through community meetings and radio messaging in addition to interpersonal communication through house-to-house visits to improve IPTp and treatment seeking among pregnant women.

Challenges, opportunities, and threats

SP is inexpensive and easily procured in Nigeria. Unfortunately, SP continues to be used for treatment of uncomplicated malaria. Patent medical vendor shops sell it for 40 naira, or about $0.32. Public health facilities in some states can order SP from state medical stores for the same price, and then charge the client for the drug. Since the goal is to provide IPTp free of charge in the public health facilities, PMI is planning to procure sufficient SP to cover FANC services in the PMI focus states. At the same time, PMI is advocating for focus states to use their own budgets to procure enough SP to cover their IPTp needs.

Table E: Sulfadoxine-pyrimethamine gap analysis for nine PMI focus states, Nigeria, 2015

PMI States*	Estimated Population 2015 (millions)	Crude Birthrate (per 1000)	ANC Attendance	Public Sector ANC	Public sector ANC women	SP treatments (4 doses)	PMI Support
Bauchi	5.9	50	15%	95%	41,769	169,163	170,000
Sokoto	4.7	50	15%	95%	33,237	134,611	135,000
Cross River	3.6	39.5	68%	80%	78,319	317,193	317,000
Nasarawa	2.4	33.1	73%	77%	43,819	177,468	177,000
Zamfara	4.1	48.5	13%	95%	24,743	100,211	100,000
Ebonyi	2.8	40	76%	55%	45,858	185,723	186,000
Benue	5.3	41.3	63%	50%	69,227	280,368	280,000
Oyo	7.0	33.3	88%	58%	119,505	483,994	484,000
Kogi	4.1	38	65%	60%	61,877	250,604	251,000
Total	39.9				518,354	2,099,335	2,100,000

The table reflects commodity gaps in the 9 original states; the two new states were added too late in the FY 2014 operational planning cycle to be included in the FY 2014 budget; these states will be included reprogramming of additional FY 2013 funding and potential new appropriations in FY 2014.

Plans and Justification

PMI will continue to support IPTp capacity building of service providers to implement FANC using directly observed treatment in PMI focus states. PMI will continue to build on the gains made in improving access to IPTp among the pregnant women who attend ANC clinics to reach the 2013 target of 80%. To expand demand for and access to IPTp services with FY 2014 funding, PMI will support mass media campaigns, innovative interpersonal communication interventions at the local government facilities and ward levels, and regular integrated supportive supervision to all facilities offering ANC services, with an increased focus on rural and hard-to-reach communities.

Description and budget for proposed activities with FY 2014 funding ($1,430,000):

1. *Procure adequate quantities of SP* for health facilities in the PMI focus states and provide other resources such as disposable cups and possibly clean water for health facilities to deliver direct observation of IPTp. ($300,000)

2. *Provide support for implementation of IPTp as part of FANC across eleven PMI focus states.* This support will include the review and update of the MIP policy document to conform with the new WHO recommendations; updating implementation guidelines and training materials; aligning the NMCP MIP policy documents with the Reproductive Health Unit policy documents; training health facility workers in each of the eleven PMI

states; periodic supportive supervision; and improved delivery of IPTp and ITNs during pregnancy. ($1,130,000)

3. *Create awareness and demand for IPTp services through BCC* in collaboration with print and electronic media. PMI will support BCC activities, including interpersonal communication, mass media, and social mobilization, to promote IPTp, as well as other key aspects of malaria control and prevention. (Costs covered under the ACSM section)

CASE MANAGEMENT

4. Diagnosis

NMCP and PMI Objectives

The Nigerian National Guidelines for Diagnosis and Treatment of Malaria are aligned with the revised 2010 WHO recommendations on universal diagnostic testing for malaria. The NMCP Strategic Plan 2009-2013 describes the general objective of achieving "timely and equitable access to malaria diagnosis and treatment by all sections of the population and as close to the home as possible." Prompt parasitological diagnosis, either by microscopy or RDT, is strongly recommended in all suspected cases of malaria.

Biological diagnosis is gradually being scaled-up in Nigeria. The target for parasitological diagnosis is 40% by 2013 and 60% by 2014. No target has yet been set for 2015. Microscopy should be available in health facilities with a high malaria case load and a need for parasite quantification and in facilities that manage other diseases needing microscopic diagnosis. The NMCP considers hospitals, large primary health centers that include inpatient beds and tertiary care facilities as the facilities where microscopy should be available. The NMCP plans to use RDTs at secondary facilities and in certain outpatient clinics of tertiary facilities when microscopy is not available.

The MIS 2010 reported that 5% of children under five with fever had a blood test taken. There was no difference between urban (5%) and rural (6%) residents. The highest level was in the North Central Zone (9%), while the lowest was in the North East (4%). The MICS 2011 reported 8% of children under five with fever had a blood test taken.

Progress during the past 12 months

The RBM partners are working to improve malaria diagnostic capacity in the public and private sectors. Laboratory technicians and microscopists are being trained at tertiary and secondary health facilities. Rapid diagnostic tests are being rolled out in primary and secondary public health facilities. Harmonized training manuals on malaria service delivery and diagnostics have been finalized and are being used.

PMI-procured RDTs began arriving in Nigeria in July 2012. A PMI End-Use Verification (EUV) survey completed in November 2012 found stockouts of RDTs at MAPS supported facilities were low, at 5% on the day of the visit. With these RDTs available, malaria diagnostics at the primary health care level has moved forward. Another EUV was recently completed in 2013. Collaboration with the Nigerian Ministry of Defense and the DOD-Walter Reed Program (DOD-WRP) on malaria diagnosis (microscopy and malaria RDT) continues. The DOD-WRP opened a new Malaria Center in Abuja that is being used for diagnostic training. PMI supported the training of 228 medical laboratory scientists in six states to date. Thirty-seven of the higher performing lab scientists were selected for training on quality assurance of malaria diagnostics. PMI supported the training of over 4000 health care providers on RDT use.

Partners are supporting the NMCP in the development of a framework for a diagnostic quality assurance (QA) system for malaria parasite diagnosis. This will be finalized soon and then used to pilot QA systems at the zonal and state levels. Implementation of the diagnostic QA system has begun using the draft National Framework and tools in Cross River and Oyo states.

A majority of Nigerians seek treatment for malaria initially through the private sector. The MIS 2010 reported that 57% of those with fever first seek treatment from a chemist or PMV. Results from a SFH 2012 study introducing RDTs to PMVs are pending. The SuNMaP is also testing approaches that will make it advantageous for these informal providers to use RDTs, both in terms of improving relations with patients and economic incentives. PMI recognizes the critical role the private sector plays in the treatment of malaria, diarrhea, and pneumonia in Nigeria and plans to proceed with pilots in three states, largely supported by USAID Maternal and Child Health funds, that involve the introduction of RDTs to PMVs for improved access to recommended case management of childhood fever.

Challenges, opportunities, and threats

With PMI-procured RDTs now available, the biggest challenge is building trust among health care providers in the results of diagnostic tests. Nigeria is similar to other sub-Saharan African countries where it is generally a challenge to get providers to follow RDT negative results. Health providers have been trained that microscopy is the "gold standard" and are not aware of the poor quality microscopy that exists in Nigeria. Providers will accept the results from a lab technician with poor training and equipment, substandard stain, and in challenging conditions over the result of a RDT with known high specificity and sensitivity. There is a great need for supportive supervision to reinforce case management training including the consideration of alternative diagnosis for RDT-negative fever cases. Professional health associations are being educated on the relevance of quality assured parasitological-based diagnosis in PMI focus states and encouraged to change their and other providers' practice behaviors accordingly. The professional groups include: the Nigerian Medical Association, the National Association of Nigeria Nurses and Midwives and the National Association of Medical Laboratory Scientists of Nigeria.

In addition, PMI Nigeria is supporting the NMCP and the State MOH in PMI focus states in diagnostic quality assurance/quality control (QA/QC). The PMI, in collaboration with DOD-WRP, provides central level train-the- trainers instruction to State MOH personnel from secondary and tertiary facilities who then conduct cascade training (on malaria diagnosis, laboratory QA/QC, and supervision) for health workers from selected facilities in the states. The trained supervisors, also MOH personnel, are then supported to conduct QA visits to all the supported health facilities and report through the state health system. This collaboration also works with the Malaria Translational Research Centre as well as the University College of Ibadan Medical School, and is assisting in the development of locally produced positive control samples for RDT QC. This is an opportunity to build confidence in RDT results using in-country capacity. This project will enhance national capacity by developing a slide bank in conjunction with the University of Ibadan that will be housed in Abuja. This bank will complement the existing one in the WHO-certified lab at the University of Lagos. PMI is leveraging PEPFAR resources which are the main funding sources for the reference laboratory in Abuja.

PMI's intent is to maintain an adequate supply of both ACTs and RDTs in selected health care facilities in the 11 focus states in order to support well-functioning facilities. With adequate supplies of commodities and the human capacity to collect and report data properly, the goal is to have these facilities provide consumption data for improved supply chain management. A threat to this approach was the possibility that states would insist on distributing PMI-procured RDTs to all public health facilities in the states, risking stockouts in PMI's priority health facilities as well as others in the state. In general this has not been the case. PMI has been able to direct commodities toward supported facilities. The greater challenge now is coordination with the Global Fund sub-recipients at the state level. Some health facilities receive support from both PMI implementing partners and Global Fund sub-recipients. Without strong coordination there is a risk that some health facilities will be overstocked with malaria commodities.

Insufficient numbers of RDTs to cover PMI-supported facilities is still a threat for FY 2013 as MAPS expands health facility coverage from four to eight facilities in all LGAs in nine supported states. With sustained higher PMI funding levels, improved partner coordination at the state level, and continued World Bank Booster Project support in Bauchi, this threat has diminished. However, the threat exists for FY 2014 by which time the World Bank Booster Project will end, Global Fund Round 8, Phase 2 will end and, for the first time, PMI Nigeria will be supporting private sector RDTs.

The expansion of the PMI-PEPFAR collaboration in Nigeria is an opportunity to increase malaria diagnostics coverage and quality. The PEPFAR funding in FY 2013 will procure RDTs for two high HIV prevalence states, Benue and Cross River. The addition of approximately 850,000 RDTs to the planned Global Fund and PMI RDTs will further improve the availability of fever case management in these two states. The plan is to work toward integrated supportive supervision in the health facilities supported by both PMI and PEPFAR. If successful, collaboration can be expanded to other states.

Commodity gap analysis

Nigeria is in the process of shifting from a parallel malaria information system to a harmonized HMIS. At the present time, case reporting through the HMIS remains poor. There are an estimated 110-150 million fever cases per year in Nigeria, with about 30% of those seeking care at public health facilities. The availability of accurate microscopy is not known, and the NMCP estimates that 50-60 million RDTs are needed annually to achieve malaria diagnostic targets in the public sector. After the initial RDT distribution to PMI supported facilities, re-supply has been based on consumption data.

The table below shows the RDT needs and gaps for 2015.

Table F: RDT gap analysis for nine PMI focus states, Nigeria, 2015

PMI States*	Est. Pop. 2015	Fevers per person/ year (0.9)	Proportion seeking treatment in the public sector (MIS 2010)	Est. RDT Need in public sector	75% public sector RDT Roll Out	Proportion seeking treatment in the private sector (MIS 2010)	20% private sector RDT Roll Out	Total Need	PMI Support	RDT Gap
				(in millions)						
Bauchi	5.9	5.3	0.30	1.6	1.2	0.70	0.7	1.9	1.6	0.4
Sokoto	4.7	4.2	0.50	2.1	1.6	0.50	0.4	2.0	1.7	0.3
Cross River	3.6	3.2	0.25	0.8	0.6	0.75	0.5	1.1	0.9	0.2
Nasarawa	2.4	2.2	0.30	0.6	0.5	0.70	0.3	0.8	0.6	0.2
Zamfara	4.1	3.7	0.50	1.8	1.4	0.50	0.4	1.8	1.4	0.4
Ebonyi	2.7	2.4	0.20	0.5	0.4	0.80	0.4	0.8	0.6	0.2
Benue	5.3	4.8	0.30	1.4	1.1	0.70	0.7	1.7	1.4	0.3
Oyo	7.0	6.3	0.25	1.6	1.2	0.75	0.9	2.1	1.7	0.4
Kogi	4.2	3.8	0.30	1.1	0.9	0.70	0.5	1.4	1.1	0.3
Total	39.9	35.9		11.6	8.7		4.9	13.6	11.0	2.6

The table reflects commodity gaps in the nine original states; the two new states were added too late in the FY 2014 operational planning cycle to be included in the FY 2014 budget; these states will be included reprogramming of additional FY 2013 funding and potential new appropriations in FY 2014.

Plans and Justification

PMI is working to develop the appropriate diagnostics package that builds capacity among health and lab personnel and supervisors. PMI will expand coverage from four to eight health facilities per LGA in the PMI focus states reaching approximately 50% coverage of facilities. In combination with Global Fund, over 70% of primary care facilities in PMI focus states are covered. The package includes not only the routine use of the tests, but also procurement, distribution, quality control, and BCC to increase client demand for testing. PMI will also continue to support the DOD-WRP which will support the training of trainers who will in turn train and supervise staff at the health facilities described above. The plan is now to begin to extend diagnostics to the private sector and community level. PMI will procure RDTs, though it will not be sufficient to cover the need in the seven MAPS states and two TSHIP states with extension into the private sector. With FY 2014 funding, PMI plans to support the following activities:

Description and budget for proposed activities with FY 2014 funding ($7,899,000):

1. *Procure an estimated 11 million RDTs.* In FY 2014 PMI will procure a sufficient number of RDTs to support the scale-up of malaria laboratory diagnosis in all 11focus states and expand into the private sector. ($4,000,000)

2. *Improve the quality of parasitological diagnosis in the public sector* through the training of health and lab personnel in 11 states. PMI will work at the state, LGA, and community level to improve the appropriate use of diagnostics including interpreting laboratory results and managing patients based on results. Support will include in-service training and supervisory visits for both laboratory workers and health-care providers as part of a comprehensive program for laboratory diagnostics. This activity began in selected health facilities in all LGAs in PMI focus states with FY 2011 funding, and expanded to additional health facilities and the community with FY 2012 and 2013 funding. With FY 2014 funding, the diagnostics package will continue to expand to additional public primary health care facility coverage in targeted states as well as further community level coverage. PMI will also continue to roll out the new malaria diagnostics QA system in PMI focus states. ($3,350,000)

3. *Improve the quality of parasitological diagnosis in the private sector* through the training of PMVs in all PMI-focus states. PMI will expand on FY 2013 supported pilot interventions that implemented Integrated Management of Childhood Illness among the PMVs in selected LGAs in three PMI-focus states in FY 2013, leveraging USAID Maternal, Newborn and Child Health (MNCH) funding. The MNCH funding will support the treatment of pneumonia and diarrhea through PMVs. ($125,000)

4. *Support for malaria diagnostic training* (microscopy and RDTs) in PMI focus states. These training activities will focus on training of trainers and refresher training in each state. These trainers will then provide training and supervision for health facilities. QA personnel will receive additional training that will strengthen QA for diagnostics at the national, zonal, and state levels. The DOD-WRP will support the roll out of RDT QC utilizing positive control wells developed through FY 2013 funding. In addition, DOD-

WRP will be used to procure supplies for quality microscopy (reagents, slides, lancets, etc.)($400,000)

5. *Technical assistance in malaria diagnostics.* The CDC will provide two technical support visits for microscopic and RDT diagnosis. ($24,000)

6. *BCC to increase patient demand for diagnostics* through activities at the community level that promote awareness of appropriate testing and treatment for malaria; and improve health-care provider adherence to test results through activities directed at health facilities. (Costs covered under the ACSM section)

5. Pharmaceutical and commodity management

NMCP and PMI Objectives

The public sector procurement and supply chain management of essential medicines is weak and fragmented. Consequently, frequent stockouts of all commodities, including ACTs, occur. Supplies of malaria-related commodities come from a variety of sources and may be donated or procured at various levels of the government health system. Donors, the federal government, states, and LGAs all can procure ACTs, SP, and RDTs. The states, LGAs, and individual health facilities can supplement donated and federal government-procured commodities by using revolving drug funds and/or oil and tax revenues. Both the sources of commodities and the distribution systems are varied. In principle, donor and government-procured essential medicines flow either through the national Central Medical Stores (CMS) to the state CMS. States often have difficulty delivering commodities to the facility level. The supply of World Bank- and Global Fund-procured ACTs has varied and resulted in stockouts in some facilities and led other facilities to acquire medicines from local pharmacies that do not always align with national policy. Many Nigerians use the private sector and local pharmacies for health care. However, the NMCP has limited capacity to oversee this sector and its production and dispensing of antimalarials without a laboratory confirmed diagnosis.

The NAFDAC is responsible for the registration of antimalarials and quality control at the point of entry for internationally procured drugs or at the factory gate for locally produced ones. This agency and the NMCP collaborate to conduct post-marketing surveillance of drugs. However, there is no WHO prequalified QC laboratory in Nigeria so the NMCP must pay outside laboratories to test medicines and other products. The country needs appropriate equipment to move NAFDAC toward meeting WHO standards for prequalification.

Progress during the past 12 months

Despite the challenges, opportunities have emerged to help ameliorate some of the problems facing Nigeria's pharmaceutical and commodity management. PMI has assisted the national and

44

state malaria control programs by establishing National Quantification Committee and Pharmaceutical Supply Management (PSM) Working Groups in the states. As a result, state-specific quantifications and gap analyses have been developed and used to inform commodity planning by partners and as advocacy tools with government counterparts.

Additionally, PMI has improved human capacity by training staff on a Malaria Commodity Logistics System. Of the 4690 public health facilities in seven PMI focus states, PMI provided training in 2025 of them. Training was conducted in 4 PMI-supported facilities and 11 Global Fund-supported facilities in each LGA of the 7 states. Two staff were trained in each of the 2025 facilities for a total of 4050 staff, of which 1080 were in PMI-supported facilities. Additionally, 212 staff were trained in 137 additional PMI-supported facilities As a result of these trainings, the availability of consumption data for decision making has increased. Such data are helping state and national malaria control staff conduct accurate forecasting and quantification, and are used to advocate with local governments for support with commodities procurement and management. Still, there remains a need to focus on improving data quality. Abuja, Lagos, and states lack sufficient storage space and in some cases have no warehouses capable of storing malaria commodities according to standard pharmaceutical guidelines (i.e., ample space, acceptable storage conditions and standard storage procedures, explicit QA mechanisms, and adequate product security). PMI continues to lease 216 pallet positions in a pharmaceutical-compliant store in Abuja. The Initiative has also identified warehouse space for ITNs in Lagos and is preparing to sign a lease close to the time of net delivery in mid-2013. Some state governments have provided storage space, but PMI has not been able to identify pharmaceutical-compliant stores in any of its supported states. While access will improve, the need for trained personnel in warehouse management will continue and is being addressed. Despite these challenges, PMI-supported facilities have been appropriately stocked, including through *ad hoc* redistribution of stocks between states, as needed.

In Ebonyi and Bauchi States, PMI and partners have designed a pilot system called DDIC to address data and distribution challenges. It involves direct delivery of commodities from the central level to facilities via trucks. At the time of delivery, a staff member on the truck checks the facility's stock, determines need using a software package, and immediately provides the needed commodities. The data are sent to headquarters where stock balances and procurement decisions are made. This model is designed to be a push or vendor-managed inventory system that is based on regular data collection, bimonthly distribution, and reporting. The goal is to achieve full supply of facilities based on the data reported. Trucks have delivered ACTs, SP, and RDTs to approximately 200 facilities in Ebonyi and plan to reach 165 in Bauchi.

PMI is also supporting the strengthening the QA/QC of antimalarials. A gap analysis of the QA/QC of medicines was conducted to help support the NAFDAC and NMCP in developing a QA/QC policy for antimalarial medicines and diagnostics.

Challenges, opportunities, and threats

Supply chain capacity and processes, including secure warehouse space and management operations, vary by state with each having its own system for managing malaria commodities in its own CMS. Additionally, there is a shortage of central and state level pharmaceutical-compliant storage space. Consequently, deliveries of the quantity needed to top up to a four-month supply at the facilities are being made close to the time of distribution and no commodities are being left at the state CMS. With multiple procurers, variable supply chains between and within states, lack of sufficient, reliable quality consumption data from all levels in the system, and weak logistics management systems in general, it is a challenge to establish a management system to track supply and develop a rational forecasting, ordering, and distribution system for malaria commodities. However, with the training provided to both national and state level staff, there is increased human capacity to help strengthen the supply chain management and increase state government support and ownership.

The DDIC pilot is promising in that it has produced more accurate forecasting and timely delivery and decreased the risk of stockouts. However, more data are needed to determine the logistics and operational costs of this approach and the potential for expansion.

PMI support for improved QA/QC of antimalarials medicines will include training staff to strengthen the regulatory capacity of NAFDAC. Also, the QA/QC enhancement will strengthen the NAFDAC's laboratory capacity.

There are also opportunities and challenges with private sector pharmaceutical producers and vendors. Various partners, including the World Bank and AMFm, have been resources for ACTs in the private sectors. The AMFm was able to register 49 first-line buyers, decrease the cost and increase the availability of quality ACTs sold by PMVs[3]. However, the target price for the subsidized ACTs could not be reached, in part because of mark-ups by intermediaries and because there were not enough ACTs available in the market. PMI is exploring options with RBM partners to build on the AMFm experience to ensure low cost quality ACTs in the private sector as donor subsidies are weaned.

While there are almost 40 registered ACTs that are manufactured in Nigeria, to date there is no producer that is WHO-prequalified for ACTs. Additionally, there are products from nonqualified foreign manufacturers, as well as artemisinin monotherapies, SP, and chloroquine in the private sector. Given the scope and size of the private sector market and its common use by many Nigerians, the NAFDAC has a difficult task when providing quality control measures in this sector.

---

[3] ACT Watch Evidence for Malaria Medicine Policy, Snapshot of Nigeria: Outlet Survey results 2009 and 2011 presentation

A threat to the availability and affordability of ACTs in the private sector exists given AMFm's end and the transition year subsidy program closing out after 2013. It is possible that fewer ACTs will be available and that they will become cost-prohibitive for some private sector users.

Plans and Justification

Given the numerous challenges with the disjointed procurement, supply, and distribution system, PMI remains committed to strengthening pharmaceutical and commodity management systems at the state level and below, ideally to the facility level. The plan is to continue to train facility staff on the LMIS and provide technical assistance to support it becoming fully operational. In this way, facilities and states will improve their ability to generate reliable data on consumption, supply, needs, and distribution of pharmaceuticals and commodities.

Description and budget for proposed activities with FY 2014 funding ($4,200,000):

1. *Strengthen the pharmaceutical and commodity management system* by improving forecasting, management, and distribution of pharmaceuticals, RDTs and ITNs, and provide warehousing and distribution of PMI-procured commodities to the facility level. This activity will help mitigate the risk of stockouts of malaria commodities and the improper disposal of expired drugs. ($4,200,000)

2. *Provide support to strengthen the national drug regulatory agency's (NAFDAC) capacity* for drug quality control, including the procurement of necessary equipment and supplies. This support will include establishing functional mini-labs that can perform key testing of drug quality in the field, providing NAFDAC with additional tools to detect fake and poor quality drugs. (Costs covered under the Treatment section)

6. Treatment

NMCP and PMI Objectives

According to the Nigerian National Guidelines for Diagnosis and Treatment of Malaria, the objective of treating uncomplicated malaria is to rapidly cure the patient to prevent progression to severe disease and reduce morbidity and mortality. In addition, prompt appropriate treatment decreases transmission and can prevent or delay the emergence of drug resistance.

In 2004 the Federal MOH changed the drug policy to ACTs with artemether-lumefantrine as the first-line treatment for uncomplicated *P. falciparum*, and artesunate–amodiaquine as the alternate first-line drug. The NMCP has established 14 sentinel sites throughout the country to monitor the efficacy of the first-line treatment. The sites utilize the WHO standardized protocol and are scheduled to conduct the studies biannually. Drug therapeutic and efficacy trials were completed at seven of these sites in 2009. The study demonstrated that adequate clinical and parasitological response on day 28 was similar for both artemether-lumefantrine (96.3%) and artesunate-amodiaquine (95.1%). The trials planned for the other seven sites in 2011 will now occur in 2013. The World Bank and Global Fund are supporting the 2013 drug trials. PMI has offered both technical and financial support for the trials if required.

The recommended treatment of uncomplicated malaria for children weighing less than five kilograms is oral quinine. Clinical malaria during pregnancy is to be treated with quinine as well, although ACTs may be used after the first trimester. For severe malaria, the Nigerian guidelines recommend intravenous (IV) or intramuscular (IM) artesunate, IV or IM quinine, or IM artemether. The recommended pre-referral treatment of severe malaria is IM or intra-rectal artesunate, quinine, or artemether.

The management of malaria in Nigeria may occur at home, in the community, or at the health facility. Initial malaria treatment is frequently sought in the private sector. The MIS 2010 found that 57% of household members first sought treatment for fever at a chemist or PMV, including 56% of children under five. Most PMVs receive some informal on-the-job training as an apprentice on the recognition of basic symptoms of uncomplicated malaria and are empowered to dispense treatment, but not perform diagnostics. Most PMVs are not aware of NMCP guidelines for malaria treatment. The NMCP is planning to expand community case management in the public sector through a community-oriented resource person. The finalization of a guideline document on community case management of malaria was put on hold while the NMCP collaborated with the Family Health Department to develop an integrated community case management document that includes malaria diagnostics with RDTs, malaria treatment with ACTs, pneumonia treatment with amoxicillin, and diarrhea treatment with zinc and ORS. The integrated community case management policy guideline has now been finalized and signed by the Minister of Health.

The MIS 2010 reports that, of children under five with fever, about 49% received any antimalarial treatment, while the MICS 2011 reports 45%. Of those children who received malaria treatment, the MIS 2010 indicates 12% took an ACT and the MICS 2011 reports 10%. In contrast, those that took chloroquine or SP were 79% in the MIS 2010 and 64% in the MICS 2011. Contributing factors to the poor uptake of ACTs include low awareness of ACT treatment by health workers and patients, frequent stockouts in public sector health facilities, and the high cost of ACTs in the private sector.

Nigeria was selected as one of nine countries to pilot the AMFm. The goal of AMFm was to reduce the retail price of ACTs to a point that they were as affordable as many of the cheapest antimalarial monotherapies. From the time the AMFm grant was signed in September 2010 until October 2012, Nigeria had AMFm orders approved for 118.2 million treatments (96.8 million private for-profit, 11.7 million public, and 9.7 million private not-for-profits) of which 98.2 million have been delivered. The AMFm ACT price in the private sector dropped from 800 –

1200 naira to a median cost of about 200 naira ($1.26) per adult dose. However, numerous antimalarial monotherapies remain on the market, including chloroquine and SP.

The AMFm Phase 1 ended as of December 2012. Nigeria has developed a plan for the transition period in 2013 which maintains ACT co-payments from external donors. PMI helped organize and facilitate an RBM partners meeting in February 2013 to review the transition plan and discuss options for 2014 onward. No consensus was reached on the continued need for a private sector subsidy in Nigeria. Strategy development continues through the Working Group on Private Sector Case Management.

Progress during the past 12 months

The NMCP, with support from SuNMaP and other partners, finalized the harmonized training manuals on malaria. Within the service delivery component, there are training manuals on malaria case management in the hospital, at the primary health care center, and for PMVs. To date PMI has supported malaria case management training of 8,600 health care providers.

The ACTs procured by PMI began arriving in country in May 2012. PMI-supported facilities in eight of the nine PMI focus states have now received ACTs. An EUV survey conducted in November 2012 showed that 100% of MAPS facilities had some kind of ACT available to treat patients. Since that survey there have been sporadic reports of stockouts of particular doses, but overall, PMI-supported facilities have continuous ACT supplies.

In the PMI focus state of Ebonyi, the DDIC pilot was initiated in January 2013 (see the Pharmaceutical and Commodity Management section for a full description). The DDIC uses trained personnel and drivers to travel to public health facilities to quantify and immediately deliver malaria commodities. The pilot will quickly expand to over 300 facilities. The PMI Nigeria is in discussion with the Global Fund to pool malaria commodities in Ebonyi for DDIC distribution.

Stockouts continue throughout large parts of the public sector. The Global Fund Round 8 Phase 2 malaria grant was signed in August 2012. The NMCP, as Global Fund Principal Recipient for the public sector, is to provide malaria commodities, including ACTs, to all 36 states and the Federal Capitol Territory of Abuja. The funding for malaria commodities over the three year period of the grant falls considerably short of the estimated need. However, the Global Fund recently announced a plus-up to $167 million for Nigeria for malaria commodities. The vast majority of this funding will go toward replacement ITNs, but funding for ACTs and RDTs is also available. The PMI-Global Fund coordination at the national level is improving and will be critical in ensuring public health facilities are adequately supplied with ACTs. PMI is in discussions with the Global Fund to distribute Global Fund-procured malaria commodities in PMI focus states.

Malaria commodity procurement by the World Bank for its six focus states is moving forward. This has a direct impact on one PMI focus state – Bauchi (population 5.6 million). Although its

Booster Program was scheduled to end in 2013, the World Bank will use remaining funding to continue to procure malaria commodities into the first quarter of 2014.

PMI supported a gap analysis of the QA/QC of medicines in Nigeria in 2013. The analysis will be used to establish an antimalarial medicines quality monitoring program in collaboration with NAFDAC and NMCP beginning in 2013. Also, through PQM/USP, PMI procured six minilabs which were delivered and trained 23 relevant staff (NAFDAC, MOH, and NMCP) to use the equipment.

The Clinton Health Access Initiative is taking the lead in advocating at the national level for injectable artesunate and is partnering with Medicines for Malaria Venture (MMV) to support implementation in six non-PMI focus states. PMI's plan to use FY 2012 funds to support the introduction of injectable artesunate in Cross River and Oyo states has been held back by procurement delays. A change in the NAFDAC-approved injection buffer necessitated restarting the procurement process. The initial order from PMI of 10,000 vials of injectable artesunate is now scheduled to arrive in August 2013, with an additional 40,000 vials in the pipeline.

Within the private sector, PMVs provide very good geographical access to many rural communities. The SFH, through Phase 1 of the Global Fund Round 8 malaria grant, introduced subsidized ACTs through pre-selected PMVs. These PMVs had agreed to a predetermined mark-up price for the ACTs. However, SFH was never able to fully supply the subsidized ACTs to the PMVs and could not evaluate this pilot due to stockouts. PMI is working with partners to develop and implement case management pilots, including using an integrated management approach, in several LGAs through PMVs in the private sector.

Challenges, opportunities, and threats

Although PMI-procured ACTs are now available at supported facilities, a malaria commodity gap still exists at the state level. Communication and coordination has improved with the Global Fund at the national level, but coordination at the state level remains a challenge. Lack of coordination could lead to oversupply of ACTs at certain facilities while others are stocked out.

PMI is advocating at the state and LGA levels for the procurement of ACTs to fill existing gaps. Some facilities procure ACTs through drug revolving funds, but these are not WHO pre-qualified ACT procurements. PMI is exploring the possibility of providing ACTs as seed stock to those facilities with drug revolving fund systems in place. If a pooled procurement mechanism were also in place, states could then build stocks of lower-cost, pre-qualified ACTs.

The intent is to maintain a supply of ACTs at PMI-supported health care facilities to demonstrate well-functioning facilities and collect accurate consumption data. As noted in the case management diagnostics section, the same concern regarding partner coordination and appropriate malaria commodity stocks at PMI supported facilities is relevant here.

The expansion of PMI-PEPFAR collaboration in Nigeria is an opportunity to increase ACT coverage. PEPFAR funding in FY 2013 will procure ACTs for two high HIV prevalence states, Benue and Cross River. The addition of approximately 1,000,000 ACTs to the planned Global fund and PMI ACTs will further improve access to malaria case management in these two states.

Commodity gap analysis

Nigeria is in the process of shifting from a parallel malaria information system to a harmonized HMIS. At this time case reporting through the HMIS remains poor. There are an estimated 110-150 million fever cases per year in Nigeria, with about 30% of those seeking care at public health facilities. After the initial ACT distribution to PMI-supported facilities, re-supply has been based on consumption data.

Table G: Estimated public and private sector ACT gap in PMI focus states, Nigeria, 2015 (in millions)

PMI States**	Est. Pop. 2015	Fevers per year (0.9)	Proportion seeking treatment in the public sector (MIS 2010)	Est. ACT Need in public sector	80 % public sector ACT roll out	RDT adjustment *	Proportion seeking treatment in the private sector (MIS 2010)	20% private sector RDT Roll Out	RDT adjustment*	Total Need	PMI Support FY14	Gap
						(in millions)						
Bauchi	5.9	5.3	0.3	1.6	1.3	0.8	0.7	0.7	0.5	1.3	1.1	0.2
Sokoto	4.7	4.2	0.5	2.1	1.7	1.1	0.5	0.4	0.3	1.4	0.9	0.5
Cross River	3.6	3.2	0.25	0.8	0.6	0.4	0.75	0.5	0.3	0.8	0.7	0.1
Nasarawa	2.4	2.2	0.3	0.6	0.5	0.3	0.7	0.3	0.2	0.5	0.5	0.0
Zamfara	4.1	3.7	0.5	1.8	1.5	1.0	0.5	0.4	0.2	1.2	0.9	0.3
Ebonyi	2.7	2.4	0.2	0.5	0.4	0.3	0.8	0.4	0.3	0.5	0.4	0.1
Benue	5.3	4.8	0.3	1.4	1.1	0.8	0.7	0.7	0.4	1.2	0.9	0.3
Oyo	7	6.3	0.25	1.6	1.3	0.8	0.75	0.9	0.6	1.5	1.2	0.3
Kogi	4.2	3.8	0.3	1.1	0.9	0.6	0.7	0.5	0.4	1.0	0.7	0.3
Total	39.9	35.9		11.6	9.3	6.2		4.9	3.2	9.4	7.3	2.1

* Based on 75% fevers tested, 40% positive for malaria, and 75% adherence to test results

*The table reflects commodity gaps in the 9 original states; the two new states were added too late in the FY 2014 operational planning cycle to be included in the FY 2014 budget; these states will be included reprogramming of additional FY 2013 funding and potential new appropriations in FY 2014.

Plans and Justification

PMI will support training and supportive supervision for case management of malaria at public health facilities and for PMVs in selected LGAs in the nine MAPS and two TSHIP states. With FY 2014 funding, MAPS will continue to expand from the original four to eight health facilities per LGA. Global Fund Round 8 Phase 2 funding will end in 2014, thus it is difficult to predict the ACT gap throughout the country, including PMI focus states, during the FY 2014 implementing period in (CY 2015). A key to sustaining progress will be advocating for states to invest their own resources in malaria commodity procurement. PMI will also support improved drug monitoring by having USP to support the Round 1 of Monitoring of Quality of Medicines for malaria commodities scheduled for October 2013.

With FY 2014 funding, PMI plans to support the following activities:

Description and budget for proposed activities with FY 2014 funding ($11,705,000):

1. *Procure ACTs and drugs for severe malaria in quantities to be determined.* Given the transition of Global Health funding, these procurements will primarily help prevent stockouts and fill gaps of antimalarial medications at public health facilities in 11 PMI focus states while also beginning to support the private sector through PMVs. ($7,800,000)

2. *Train and provide supportive supervision for case management at public health facilities* in nine MAPS and two TSHIP states with increasing effort at the community level. Improvement of malaria case management in the public sector will focus on increasing training and motivation of the health workers. At the community level, PMI will work with the NMCP and relevant partners to improve the rollout of integrated community case management of childhood illnesses. PMI will continue the roll out of injectable artesunate in 11 PMI focus states. ($3,430,000)

3. *Improve the quality of malaria case management in the private sector* through the training of PMVs in PMI focus states. Building on pilots for Integrated Management of Childhood Illness undertaken in selected LGAs in three states in FY 2013, PMI will expand to additional states, leveraging USAID MNCH funding. The MHNC resources will support the treatment of pneumonia and diarrhea through the PMVs. ($125,000)

4. *Provide support to strengthen the national drug regulatory agency's (NAFDAC) capacity* for drug quality control, including the procurement of necessary equipment and supplies. This support will include NAFDAC establishing six functional mini-labs in the six geopolitical zones that can perform key tests for drug quality in the field and provide NAFDAC with additional tools to detect fake and poor quality drugs. ($350,000)

5. *Support BCC activities to improve treatment-seeking behavior and treatment adherence* through interpersonal communication, community awareness and mobilization, and radio

messaging. (Costs covered under the Advocacy, Communication and Social Mobilization (ACSM) section)

CROSS CUTTING

7. Advocacy, communication, and social mobilization

NMCP and PMI Objectives

The RBM partners, under the leadership of the NMCP, have revised and updated the National Malaria ACSM Strategic Framework and Implementation Plan. The framework and plan are consistent with the NMCP Strategic Plan 2009-2013. The strategic framework is designed to provide an integrated communication plan that standardizes messages and tools for all partners with the understanding that states may need to adapt it to their particular situation. The strategic framework recommends various channels of communication based on specific attributes of the target audiences, such as literacy levels, access to television or radio, and other social and economic characteristics. The objective of these interventions is to increase and/or improve ITN ownership and net care, repair, and use; patient demand for diagnostics by promoting awareness of appropriate testing and treatment for malaria; health-care provider adherence to test results through activities directed at health facilities; delivery of IPTp at the facility level; and treatment seeking behavior and treatment adherence. In general, households and families are reached using radio, community drama, printed materials, community and religious leaders, and through community support groups and household visits of volunteers IPC.

The National Malaria ACSM branch is one of the six branches of the NMCP and is supported by the ACSM technical sub-committee. Members of the technical committee are drawn from RBM partners including PMI. The ACSM technical sub-committee plays critical roles in revising the strategic framework, helping develop tools, and assisting in coordinating activities across RBM partners. It also reviews the technical content of all BCC messages pertaining to malaria to ensure their accuracy and harmonization.

At the state level, the BCC program liaises with the state malaria focal person. In PMI focus states, the state malaria focal persons are supported by states' ACSM technical committees, which were recently established with PMI support.

Progress during the past 12 months

PMI supports BCC as a cross-cutting activity focusing on all interventions: case management, including diagnostics, ITNs, and IPTp. Implementation is principally through PMI implementing partners MAPS and TSHIP, which work in the 11 PMI focus states, and Expanded Social Marketing Program in Nigeria , which has interpersonal communication activities in 4 of the 11 focus states and nationwide through mass media. Activities include increasing and improving the information delivered by facility-based and community health workers, use of local language radio transmission to disseminate malaria messages on malaria prevention and treatment, and use of Interpersonal Communication through volunteers at the community level. PMI also supports radio shows in Hausa through Voice of America, which covers many of these same issues and reaches a large listenership across much of northern Nigeria. The Voice of America also works with journalists to identify and develop appropriate malaria news.

In 2012, PMI reached approximately 1.5 million individuals with BCC messages on ITN use; over 9,000 individuals with BCC messages on antenatal care and intermittent preventive treatment of malaria; and over 8,500 individuals with BCC messages on prompt care seeking for fever and severe malaria for children under five.

PMI continued to support quarterly meetings of the six state ACSM committees and Ward Development Committees (WDCs) to improve the quality of BCC activities in communities and at all levels of the states' health systems, as well as to enhance coordination across line ministries, donors, implementing partners, and the private sector. Advocacy with the private sector resulted in the appointment of one of Nigeria's most successful businessmen as Malaria Ambassador. In April 2013, PMI finalized grant agreements with six community-based organizations. The community-based organizations conduct IPC activities at the household level in four states – Benue, Nasarawa, Cross River and Zamfara. Additional community-based organization grants are being finalized, which will expand coverage to three additional states. The scope of work for the additional community-based organization grants will include intensifying community level interventions for malaria prevention, case management and malaria in pregnancy.

PMI supported the update of the National Advocacy Kit to harmonize malaria messages. The National Advocacy Kits are a collection of policy briefs that were developed by NMCP-led malaria partners. After the development of the Advocacy, Communication and Social Mobilization Strategic Framework and Implementation Plan, the kits were developed to ensure uniformity of messages being used to advocacy. Partners are encouraged to use the materials, though they require periodic updates with data.

PMI continues to support the ongoing operations research on approaches to promote net care and repair. Additionally, PMI supported a study on the social, cultural, and economic factors that serve as barriers to uptake of IPTp in two states, Cross River and Nasarawa. The study confirmed significant gaps between ANC attendance and uptake of IPTp among pregnant women. Additionally, the study identified social and community factors – such as the support or disapproval of spouses or partners, relatives and friends – that affect women's health-seeking behavior relating to MIP. Uptake of IPTp is also constrained by perceptions of rude and unfriendly attitudes of health workers and system factors, such as long waits and the requirement to pay for prescription drugs. Further, front-line health workers indicated they do not have sufficient training and experience in focused antenatal care that integrates malaria prevention and treatment. The study report recommended communication programs to mobilize communities as a whole, rather than seeking to change individual behavior in piecemeal fashion and hoping for "trickle-down" or "trickle-up" effects.

Challenges, opportunities, and threats

Challenges: Misperceptions, lack of knowledge, and poor practices related to malaria are common in Nigeria. While awareness about malaria transmission has increased, many misconceptions persist. Although 82% of women interviewed in the MIS 2010 identified mosquitoes as a source of malaria, common misconceptions persist as other causes cited include dirty surroundings (27%), the presence of stagnant water (12%), and eating certain foods (6%). Among children under five treated for malaria in the two weeks preceding the survey, only 6% took an ACT, while 29% took chloroquine. Antenatal clinic attendance is low; only 58% of women received ANC from a skilled provider, and only 17% received two doses of IPTp. These data point to the need for increased and more effective BCC for malaria prevention and control.

Opportunities: The vibrant and independent media in Nigeria provides opportunities to reach the public. Over 120 local radio stations exist nationwide and they can be found in all states, with heavier concentrations in the urbanized areas. Local radio stations broadcast in the range of local languages, providing opportunity for targeted communications. According to the MIS 2010, 30% of women surveyed had heard a message about malaria in the previous four weeks. Of these women, 63% heard them on the radio, while 39% reported seeing them on television. Overall, in rural areas, women more frequently heard the message on radio (74%), while in urban areas women more frequently saw messages on television (45%).

Various types of community structures provide opportunities to promote BCC in the communities. The robust local, cultural, traditional, and religious gatherings provide opportunities to reach rural communities. For example, community meetings and sermons delivered in places of worship have created more opportunities for BCC messages to be disseminated to a large number of individuals.

Plans and Justification

PMI will continue to support the BCC efforts of the NMCP and state malaria control programs to create demand for malaria diagnosis before treatment, treatment with ACTs as the drug of choice, IPTp for pregnant women, and nightly use of ITNs for prevention of malaria. The MIS 2010 results indicate that mass media is effective in reaching the target population, with 63% of women having received key malaria message through the radio and 39% through television. PMI will continue to support dissemination through these mass media channels as well as household-level IPC. PMI will evaluate the effect of BCC activities on utilization of interventions. The evaluation will build on existing data and collect intermediate results. The evaluation will use qualitative methods such as focus group discussions and key informant interviews to assess knowledge and attitude changes based on the malaria messages. Additionally, the 2014 MIS will provide quantitative measurements of behavioral change in target states.

Starting with ITNs, PMI will support communication on ITN care and use after mass campaigns, with increasing association with continuous delivery. As PMI scales up improvements to case management and IPTp, health-care workers will increasingly become important agents for promoting ITNs, IPTp, and ACTs to their patients. Additionally, PMI will strengthen the integration of BCC messaging in the health-care setting with efforts to expand the role of community health workers as active promoters of ITNs, IPTp, and ACTs.

Description and budget for proposed activities with FY 2014 funding ($2,550,000):

1. *Support a combination of BCC and social marketing* that will include intense IPC activities in four PMI focus states (Oyo, Zamfara, Bauchi, and Sokoto) and mass media nationwide using radio, drama, and magazines produced in four languages for messages on diagnosis and treatment of malaria, ITN ownership and use, and uptake of IPTp. This funding includes an evaluation of the success of interventions. PMI will also support social marketing for ACTs and ITNs, as part of a mixed-model strategy to increase ITN availability. The social marketing campaign is not a branded campaign and therefore should not interfere with the more general BCC messages that PMI fosters. ($1,000,000)

2. *Support BCC using IPC and mass media for malaria prevention, diagnosis, and treatment* across its 11 focus states. This funding targets malaria messaging to the most vulnerable groups to increase care-seeking behavior and promote the ownership and use of ITNs. This BCC is targeted in the 11 PMI states and is focused only on malaria. This support is complementary to activities supported above. ($1,400,000) ($1,400,000)

3. *Support advocacy for malaria prevention and control* through the mass media, including collaboration with journalists, to identify and develop appropriate malaria topics for reporting. ($150,000)

8. Monitoring and evaluation/operations research

NMCP and PMI Objectives

In 2009, the NMCP developed the National Monitoring and Evaluation Plan for Malaria Control in Nigeria. The process was led by the NMCP's M&E Technical Working Group and was supported by a broad group of partners including Global Fund, WHO, World Bank, UNICEF, USAID, DfID, and local non-governmental organizations. The plan covers three main areas: strengthening routine data systems, strengthening periodic household surveys, and improving operations research to ensure new intervention strategies are evidence-based. The plan was updated in 2011 with the M&E Plan for Malaria Control in Nigeria 2011-2013.

PMI's M&E approach in Nigeria fits within the framework of the National Malaria Monitoring and Evaluation Plan. Specifically, PMI supports strengthening routine data systems at various levels of the health system; periodic population-based surveys such as the MIS and the DHS to measure the status of key malaria indictors; and operations research to guide programmatic decisions.

The dual approach to collecting routine malaria data, comprised of the national HMIS managed by the Federal MOH's Health Information Unit, and the parallel malaria reporting system, established in response to Global Fund requirements and managed by the NMCP, is being phased out. This system was implemented in all 36 states and the Federal Capital Territory of Abuja with varying degrees of success. This malaria-specific information system required that only the ten Global Fund-supported health facilities per LGA report malaria data on a monthly basis to the LGA. National HMIS data are to be reported monthly from health facilities to the LGA level. The LGA HMIS focus persons collate and summarize these data quarterly and submit reports to their respective states. The state HMIS office collates data from the LGAs and reports to the national HMIS coordinator on a biannual basis. Historically, reporting of these data has been incomplete.

The WHO State Coordinator collects data on a monthly basis from the Infectious Disease Surveillance Report on 40 infectious diseases including malaria cases. Though reporting is still incomplete, this system covers more health facilities than the malaria reporting system managed by the NMCP.

Progress during the past 12 months

In April 2012, the Department of Health Planning, Research & Statistics held a stakeholders' workshop to harmonize all data collection and reporting tools into one HMIS. The NMCP and malaria partners participated in the process that produced the new HMIS tools. The Global Fund supports the harmonized HMIS for the collection of epidemiologic data and expects the LMIS to provide data on malaria commodities. With partner support, the harmonized HMIS tools are being gradually implemented in 2013. PMI assisted in developing the instructional manual and trainer guide and supported the national training of trainers in Abuja. This national team of HMIS trainers will support the rollout of the HMIS to the states.

The national platform for the electronic HMIS is the District Health Information System (DHIS). PMI provided technical support to commence implementation in PMI-supported states. The Department of Planning, Research and Statistics (DPRS) in each state organized a team of health data stakeholders to coordinate financial and technical support.

Figure 4: Proposed harmonized HMIS system

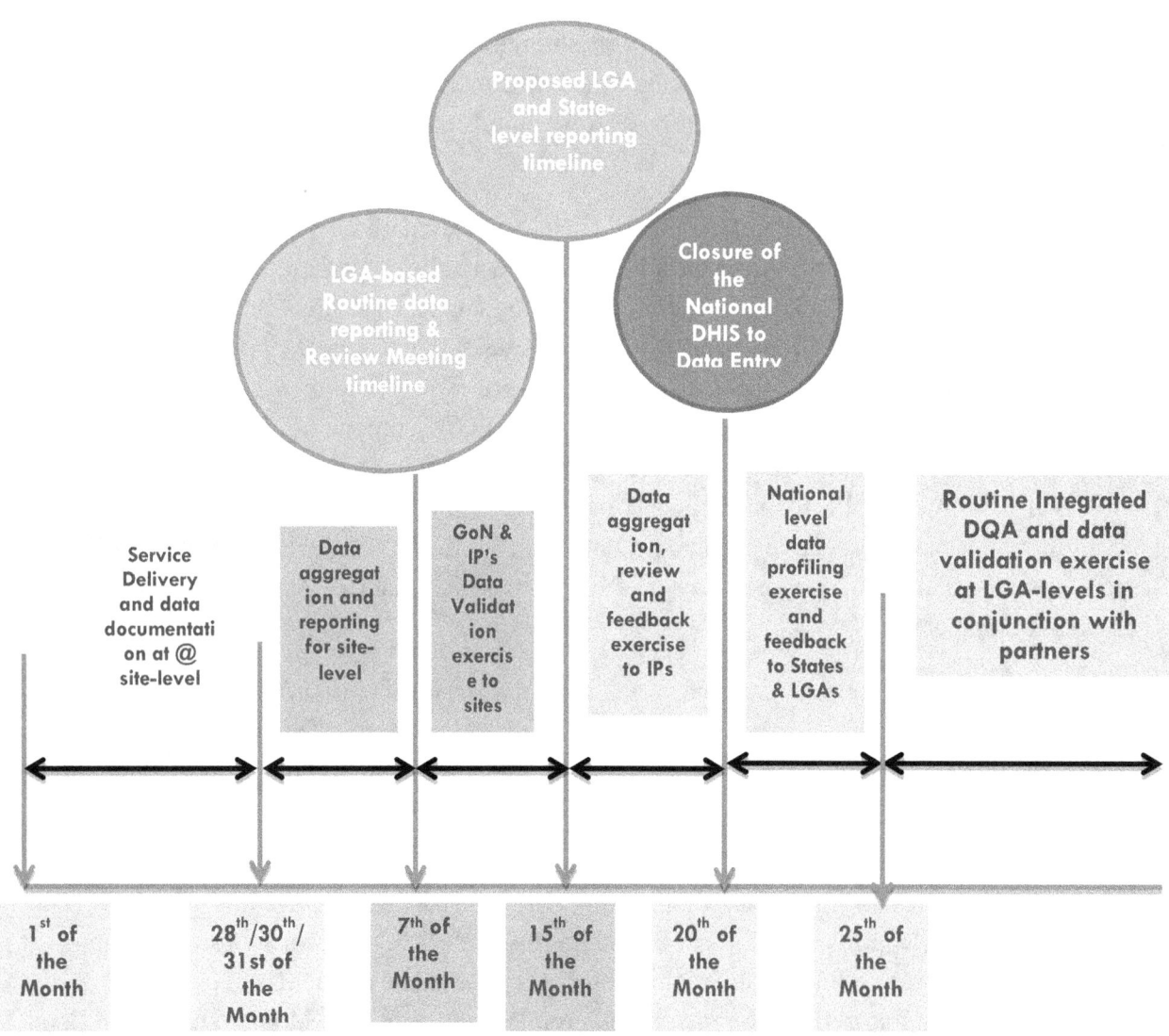

Phases I to III of the 2012 Malaria Program-performance Review (MPR) have been completed. The final report is pending, but will document findings along nine thematic areas: epidemiology; program management; policies and strategies; integrated vector management; case management; malaria in pregnancy; procurement and supply management; advocacy, communication and social mobilization; malaria in complex emergencies; and surveillance, monitoring and evaluation and operations research. The report will provide direction for developing the new five-year malaria strategic plan.

PMI is supporting the Nigeria DHS 2013, with data collection occurring from February to June 2013. National preliminary results could be available by September 2013, but final state level information will take longer. The malaria module is included in the survey but without biomarkers.

The NMCP in collaboration with the Malaria Consortium, the Malaria Atlas Project-Africa initiative, and the WHO country office developed a series of malaria risk maps to help understand the impact of recent control investments and chart the future requirements necessary to accelerate impact. Developed through a detailed modeling exercise based on parasite prevalence rates, rainfall and other factors, these maps (shown below) may demonstrate a shift of potential malaria risk over time from eastern to western Nigeria, possibly due to malaria program interventions. Nevertheless, the malaria risk remains relatively high nationwide.

Figure 5: A description of the epidemiology of malaria 2000, 2005 and 2010 to guide the planning of control in Nigeria - National Malaria Control Programme, Abuja, Nigeria January 2013

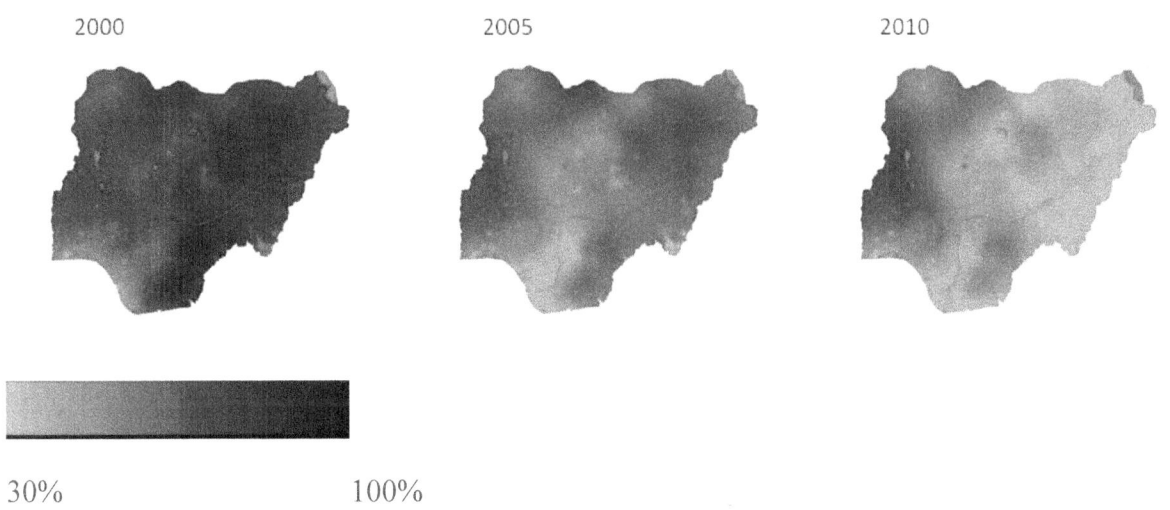

Since FY 2011 PMI has supported MOH staff participation in the Nigeria Field Epidemiology and Laboratory Training Program (FELTP). This program builds needed expertise and skills in epidemiologic principles and concepts and leads to improvements in data collection and use by NMCP and state-level M&E staff. The FELTP residents will support the monitoring of malaria burden in the PMI focus states and ultimately assist in measuring the impact of program scale-up on malaria morbidity and mortality. Previously three malaria residents graduated from the program with PEPFAR support. After completion of the program, one of the graduates was deployed to the NMCP in the case management unit and mentors other residents. The other two graduates are posted at State MOH and mentor FELTP residents posted to SMCPs of Kaduna, Oyo, Nasarawa and Kogi. FY 2011 funding was leveraged with PEPFAR funding to support three residents: one posted at the Federal MOH/NMCP M&E unit, and two at state ministries of health in Oyo and Nasarawa. The residents are being supported and mentored to develop proposals for operations research addressing key malaria interventions identified by the NMCP.

With 2012 funding, the program is supporting four residents to focus on malaria at the NMCP and three PMI-supported states (Zamfara, Ebonyi and Benue).

Table H: Malaria Data Sources, Nigeria, 2010-2015

Data Source	Year					
	2010	2011	2012	2013	2014	2015
Household Surveys: national	MIS*	MICS*	NARHS***	DHS	MIS	
Household Surveys: sub-national	World Bank* (9 states)	MABA** (7 states)				
Other Surveys			EUV#	RIA##		
Malaria Surveillance and routine system support			HMIS	HMIS	HMIS	HMIS
* Report and dataset are available.						
** MABA – Malaria and Anthropometric Baseline Assessments						
***NARHS - National AIDS and Reproductive Health Survey						
# EUV – End Use Verification						
## RIA – Rapid Impact Assessment						

Achieving timely and complete data collection and reporting on malaria from the health facility to the LGA and then to the state and national levels continues to be a challenge. Poor reporting at the facility level is the result of several factors: poor training, lack of motivation, confusion over multiple reporting forms, no supportive supervision, and essentially no accountability or feedback. The new harmonized HMIS is an opportunity to greatly improve the availability of consistent malaria information. The transition to the one single HMIS will take time to complete and success will vary from state to state. PMI supports M&E personnel in the 11 focus states who are facilitating the harmonization process. PMI will also be seconding M&E staff to the NMCP and the DPRS in four states. However, the likelihood of success is low if malaria partners alone promote the harmonized HMIS; collaboration with other stakeholders (MNCH, Reproductive health/family planning, HIV/AIDS, tuberculosis) is critical.

Nigeria conducted three national surveys (MIS 2010, MICS 2011, and NARHS 2012) that have included malaria modules. The NARHS 2012 results are not currently available. Once the DHS 2013 is completed and results are available, an opportunity exists to follow Nigeria's progress in malaria program scale up and coverage from 2010 – 2013 and identify future program directions.

Plans and Justification

Monitoring and evaluating PMI's activities will rely on a combination of routine malaria data collection, household surveys, and information from partners. With FY 2014 funds, PMI will provide support to strengthen routine malaria data collection at the health facility, LGA, and state levels through the harmonized HMIS. The objective is to achieve 100% on-time reporting of malaria cases by LGAs and 80% by functioning health facilities in PMI focal states. With FY 2014 funds, PMI intends to support the following activities:

Description and budget for proposed activities with FY 2014 funding ($2,434,000):

1. *Strengthen routine M&E systems in 11 focus states:* PMI will help strengthen the harmonized HMIS at health facility, LGA, and state levels in nine MAPS and two TSHIP states. Implementation activities will include: training and supervision of data clerical staff at selected health facilities, LGAs, and states; completion of unified data collection formats; and improving collection and reporting of routine malaria indicators. Activities will include an assessment of malaria core indicators, and an evaluation of reporting systems at all levels to include a review of completeness and timeliness of malaria reporting. Activities will be conducted in collaboration with WHO and other partners to ensure that harmonized data indicators and reports are used nationally. Data analysis, use, and dissemination at the LGA, state, and national levels will also be a priority. ($1,910,000)

2. *Support for FELTP*: Support training of five NMCP and/or state-level staff in epidemiologic methods, data analysis techniques, operations research, and strategic information for public health decision making through Nigeria FELTP. ($500,000)

3. *Technical Assistance for M&E strengthening*: CDC will provide two in-country technical assistance visits to strengthen M&E during FY 2014. ($24,000)

4. *Entomological monitoring for insecticide resistance*: Entomologic monitoring will guide the selection of insecticides by others undertaking IRS and provide information on resistance to pyrethroids used in ITNs. (Costs covered under the IRS section)

5. *Operations research*: Scaling up of the evidenced-based successes of operations research supported in FY 2012 and FY 2013 will be the focus of FY 2014. These include assessing the durability of ITNs, determining the most appropriate continuous distribution channels, and evaluating efforts to improve ITN care and repair in Nigeria. (Costs covered under the ITN section)

NMCP and PMI Objectives

The Nigerian approach to malaria control is part of the revised and comprehensive health policy founded on strengthening the overall health system to reach the MDGs.

Global Fund, World Bank, and other donors have been contributing primarily to building capacity at federal MOH level. PMI, DfID, the SuNMaP project, and Global Fund provide support to the NMCP to organize coordination meetings with partners and conduct trainings. These partners also help build capacity at the state, LGA, and facility levels. Technical expertise varies greatly across states and LGAs, as does program management and M&E expertise. PMI focuses on strengthening state and LGA abilities to plan, budget, implement, supervise, monitor, and evaluate their malaria control and prevention efforts in the 11 PMI focus states.

Additionally, PMI strengthens workforce capacity by supporting selected candidates in the CDC Nigeria FELTP. The NMCP and SMCPs identify promising individuals to earn a Master of Public Health degree and complete experiential and didactic learning opportunities during a two–year fellowship. During their training, the fellows strengthen their applied epidemiological skills and practice, especially in the area of malaria prevention and control.

Progress during the past 12 months

PMI has supported training, refresher training, supportive supervision, provision of job aids, and other activities to improve delivery of malaria interventions in 1,456 primary health care and secondary health facilities in 11 PMI focus states. In Bauchi, integrated community case management was advanced by implementing community-directed interventions and designing a pilot program to improve case management using PMVs. Registered by the Pharmaceutical Council of Nigeria, the PMVs in Bauchi are a potential resource for improving case management.

In seven states, PMI trained 925 health workers and 114 community health workers in malaria case management, and 423 health workers in the use of RDTs. These were followed up with "On the Job Capacity Building" and supervisory visits to facilities. In two other states, PMI enhanced workforce capacity by training 4,537 health service providers in malaria prevention and case management. Management and planning skills have been improved through the development of state malaria strategies, annual work plans, training plans, and costed operational plans, in consultation with state ministries of health staff. Rapid assessments of the management of malaria control in four PMI focus states have improved malaria program management capacity at the state and LGA levels. These activities have been supported by the state malaria partners' coordinating body, which includes state technical working groups for case management, communication, and monitoring and evaluation. In addition, PMI is strengthening the harmonized National Health Information System in PMI focus states by integrating malaria data elements into the tools. Other support includes working with NMCP and other Nigerian government entities to build capacity for M&E and for operations research, as seen in the government participation in population-based surveys such as the MIS, and pilot studies on net care and repair, ITNs durability, and innovative ITN distribution approaches.

PMI has also helped strengthen entomological monitoring capacity, particularly for monitoring insecticide resistance, and trained over 350 personnel in both the techniques of spraying insecticides for IRS and in overall management of IRS operations in IRS-focus LGAs. The training should improve the capacity of local and state officials to assume IRS operations, in which PMI is no longer involved.

PMI has supported three to four FELTP residents each year, with five being the latest class size. The residents have worked at SMCPs gaining valuable on-the-job-training and at the same time providing needed personnel support for surveillance, epidemiological and program management activities.

Challenges, opportunities and threats

Challenges: The Nigerian government's primary health care services remain weak. Observations by PMI Resident Advisors during field visits and available data indicate that public primary health care facilities have inadequate stocks of pharmaceuticals and support services, are not properly maintained, do not regularly pay their staff's salaries, and have inadequate record keeping. Additionally, despite training, providers' lack of confidence in RDT results and prescribing preferences are affecting rational use of ACTs. Redeployment of trained staff and the absence of specific job descriptions negatively impact human resource capacity, management systems, and quality of service delivery.

Opportunities: A dynamic private sector offers an opportunity to fill part of the gap left by a weak primary health care system. The private sector represents an important share of health-care provision in Nigeria. This sector includes pharmacists and PMVs, outpatient clinics, private doctors, and hospitals. There is an opportunity the sector will help to ensure better public/private partnerships in the provision of health care. Additionally, the piloting and uptake of integrated community case management is another opportunity to strengthen the health system and case management.

Plans and justification

Given the large size of Nigeria's population, decentralized health system, and multiple donors, it is critical for the NMCP to coordinate activities and resources so they may be used efficiently. Additionally, it is important for states to have the capacity to do the same. Consequently, PMI will support strengthening technical capacity and coordination. In view of the continued support for the FELTP program from CDC, NMCP, and SMCP, PMI will continue its support for this program. With each graduating class, the cadre of trained epidemiologists increases with focused expertise in malaria.

Description and budget for proposed activities with FY 2014 funding ($500,000):

1. *Support to the NMCP to strengthen technical capacity and national level coordination of the malaria program.* PMI will support the NMCP's role as the lead coordination body through meeting support, supervision support, and training. PMI will also provide support to 11 states to plan, implement, and monitor their malaria control programs. This may include support for workshops, travel, technical assistance to states, and other related activities. ($500,000)

2. *Technical assistance* through PMI in-country staff for project coordination, programming, partnership, and managing of malaria projects, malaria-related policies, and guidelines dissemination. (Costs covered under Staffing and Administration section)

3. *Support to states and LGAs* through implementing partners PMI will strengthen supportive supervision by state and LGA workers. (Costs covered across Case Management, IPTp and ITN sections.)

4. *Support the FELTP.* The PMI will support five FELTP trainees. (Costs covered under the M&E section)

10. Staffing and administration

During 2013 there was a complete change in the PMI field staff with the arrival of two new Resident Advisors, one from CDC and one from USAID, and two senior-level Foreign Service National staff. All PMI staff members are part of a single interagency team led by the USAID Mission Director or his/her designee in country. The PMI team shares responsibility for development and implementation of PMI strategies and work plans, coordination with national authorities, managing collaborating agencies and supervising day-to-day activities.

The four PMI professionals work together to oversee all technical and administrative aspects of PMI, including finalizing details of the project design, implementing malaria prevention and treatment activities, monitoring and evaluation of outcomes and impact, and reporting of results. All PMI staff members report to the USAID Mission Director or his/her designee. The CDC Resident Advisor is supervised by CDC both technically and administratively. All technical activities are undertaken in close coordination with the federal MOH and respective state MOHs and other national and international partners, including the WHO, UNICEF, the Global Fund, DfID, World Bank, and the private sector.

Locally-hired staff to support PMI activities either in Ministries or in USAID will be approved by the USAID Mission Director. Because of the need to adhere to specific country policies and

USAID accounting regulations, any transfer of PMI funds directly to Ministries or host governments will need to be approved by the USAID Mission Director and Controller.

Description and budget for proposed activities with FY 2014 funding ($2,400,000):

1. *In-country staff and administrative costs* for oversight to the PMI malaria activities and technical assistance to the NMCP. ($2,400,000)

IV. TABLES

Table 1. Budget Breakdown by Partner

Partner Organization	Geographic Area	Activity	Total Budget, by Partner	% of Total
DELIVER	11 PMI focus states	Procure and deliver ITNs, ACTs, drugs for severe malaria, RDTs, SP for IPTp.	$37,277,000	62%
IRS IQC T01	Federal and State level	Strengthen entomological monitoring and capacity at federal and state levels.	$1,000,000	2%
TSHIP/TBD	2 TSHIP states	Support malaria service delivery; increase diagnostic and treatment capacity of health workers at facility and community level, including private sector Patent Medicine Vendors; strengthen HMIS reporting.	$2,620,000	4%
MAPS	9 MAPS states and Federal NMCP	Support malaria service delivery; increase diagnostic and treatment capacity of health workers at facility and community level, including private sector Patent Medicine Vendors; strengthen HMIS reporting; support to the NMCP to strengthen capacity and leadership role.	$11,050,000	18%
MAPS Follow-on	9 MAPS states	Support malaria service delivery; increase diagnostic and treatment capacity of health workers at facility and community level, including private sector Patent Medicine Vendors; strengthen HMIS reporting.	$2,700,000	4%
CDC-IAA	Federal and State level	CDC TDYs to support, entomology, M&E, and case management activities; support for FELTP for five NMCP personnel.	$603,000	1%
NetWorks follow-on	11 PMI focus states	Support scaling up of evidence-based continuous distribution and care and repair approaches in PMI focus states.	$300,000	0%
VOA	Nationwide	Support for mass media for malaria prevention and control, including working with journalists to improve coverage of malaria issues.	$150,000	0%
ESMPIN	Nationwide (with a focus in MAPS and TSHIP states)	Support for BCC and Social Marketing with IPC activities in four PMI focus states and mass media nationwide addressing issues related to all major malaria interventions.	$1,000,000	2%
USP	Nationwide	Strengthen NAFDAC capacity for drug quality control including support for mini-labs to perform drug quality testing in the field.	$350,000	1%
Malaria Care	11 PMI focus states	Scale up interventions to improve integrated management of childhood illness to all PMI focus states.	$250,000	0%
WRAIR (DOD)	11 PMI focus states	Support roll out of diagnostic and QA for diagnostics to ll PMI focus states.	$400,000	1%
USAID/CDC	Nationwide	Support for USAID and CDC annual staffing and administration costs.	$2,400,000	4%
		TOTAL	$60,100,000	100%

Table 2. FY 2014 Nigeria Planned Obligations

Proposed Activity	Mechan-ism	Total Budget	Commodi-ties	Geogra-phic area	Description of Activity
ITNs					
Procure approximately 5.1 million ITNs.	DELIVER	$20,977,000	$18,477,000	11 states: 9 MAPS states and 2 TSHIP states	Procure and deliver approximately 5.1 million ITNs: 4.3 million ITNs to support universal coverage campaigns in Cross River and Zamfara states and about .8 million for continuous delivery, keep-up approaches in other PMI focus states.
Logistic and operational support for distribution of ITNs.	MAPS	$2,450,000	$0	9 states under the MAPS project	Support for delivery of about 4.3 million ITNs through a mass campaign in two PMI focus states and about 1.5 million through continuous distribution approaches in other PMI focus states with the goal of maintaining high ITN coverage.
	MAPS/ Follow-on	$700,000	$0	9 states under the MAPS project	
	TSHIP/ TBD	$1,500,000	$0	2 TSHIP states	
Technical assistance	TBD	$300,000	$0	11 PMI focus states	Technical support for scaling up of evidence-based continuous distribution, and care and repair approaches in all PMI focus states if results of research are positive.
Subtotal ITNs		***$25,927,000***	***$20,977,000***		
IRS					
Provide support for vector surveillance and susceptibility monitoring in six geopolitical zones around Nigeria.	IRS IQC T01	$550,000	$50,000	Nasarawa	Supervision, entomologic monitoring, per diem, vehicle rentals and equipment necessary to survey malaria vectors in six geopolitical zones throughout the country to determine vector species, seasonality, parity rates, indoor densities six times/year and insecticide susceptibility status to four classes of insecticide once/year.
Strengthen capacity of entomological expertise at federal and state levels.	IRS IQC T01	$450,000	$65,000	Federal and State level	Strengthen capacity of entomological competence at federal and state levels with training and equipment support to include to State Vector Control Officers and NMCP staff.

Technical assistance (TA) to PMI IRS activities.	CDC IAA	$55,000	$19,000	Federal and State level	Three CDC TDYs ($12,000/each) to provide support for IRS and resistance test kits for 40 Nigerian staff attending training.
Subtotal: IRS		*$1,055,000*	*$134,000*		

IPTp

Procure adequate quantities of SP	DELIVER	$300,000	$300,000	11 states: 9 MAPS states and 2 TSHIP states	The PMI will procure about three million treatments of SP to meet the needs for IPTp in eleven states.
Provide support for implementation of IPTp as part of FANC across all eleven PMI focus states.	MAPS	$800,000	$0	9 states under the MAPS project	Provide support for implementation of IPTp as part of FANC across all eleven PMI focus states, which will include support for the review and update of the MIP policy document, implementation guidelines, and the training materials of the NMCP in collaboration with the Division of Reproductive Health, as well as improved delivery of IPTp and ITNs during pregnancy.
	MAPS/ Follow-on	$200,000	$0	9 states under the MAPS project	
	TSHIP/ TBD	$130,000	$0	2 TSHIP states	
Subtotal: IPTp		*$1,430,000*	*$300,000*		

Case Management

Diagnostics

Procure an estimated 11 million RDTs	DELIVER	$4,000,000	$4,000,000	11 states: 9 MAPS states and 2 TSHIP states	Procure about 11 million RDTs to fill gaps and help prevent stockouts of malaria diagnostic tests in the public sector in eleven states.
Improve the quality of parasitological diagnosis in the public sector	MAPS	$2,800,000		9 MAPS states	Strengthen parasitological diagnosis with microscopy and RDTs in all eleven PMI focus states. Principal interventions will be training and supportive supervision at secondary and primary health care facilities.
	MAPS/ Follow-on	$300,000		9 MAPS states	
	TSHIP/ TBD	$250,000	$0	2 TSHIP states	

Improve the quality of parasitological diagnosis in the private sector	Malaria Care	$125,000	$0	11 states: 9 MAPS states and 2 TSHIP states	Build on the pilots interventions for Improved Case Management of Childhood Illness that were undertaken in selected LGAs in three PMI-supported states with FY 2013 funding. Best practices will be scaled-up to additional PMI focus states.
Support for malaria diagnostic training	Walter Reed Army Institute of Research	$400,000	$0	11 states: 9 MAPS states and 2 TSHIP states	WRAIR training activities will focus on training of trainers in each state, who will then roll out training to the health facilities. QA for diagnostics at the national, zonal, and state levels will also be strengthened.
TA in malaria diagnostics	CDC IAA	$24,000	$0	Nationwide	Two CDC TDYs to provide technical support to microscopic and RDT diagnosis of malaria.
Subtotal Diagnostics		*$7,899,000*	*$4,000,000*		
Pharmaceutical Management					
Strengthen the pharmaceutical and commodity management system	DELIVER	$4,200,000	$0	11 states: 9 MAPS states and 2 TSHIP states	Strengthen the pharmaceutical management system, forecasting, management and distribution of pharmaceuticals and RDTs and provide warehousing and distribution of PMI-procured commodities to the facility level. This activity will help mitigate the risk of stockouts of malaria commodities and the improper disposal of expired drugs.
Subtotal: PSM		*$4,200,000*	*$0*		
Treatment					
Procure ACTs and severe malaria drugs in quantities to be determined.	DELIVER	$7,800,000	$7,800,000	11 states: 9 MAPS states and 2 TSHIP states	Procure ACTs to fill gaps and help prevent stockouts of antimalarial medications in the public sector in eleven PMI focus states while also beginning to support the private sector through PMVs
Train and provide supportive supervision for case management at public health	MAPS	$2,200,000	$0	9 MAPS states	Improve malaria case management in the public sector, with a focus on training and motivation of the health workers. At the community level PMI support the use of
	MAPS/ Follow-on	$850,000		9 MAPS states	

facilities	TSHIP/ TBD	$380,000	$0	2 TSHIP States	innovative strategies to improve the roll out of integrated community case management of childhood illnesses through CHWs and PMVs.
Improve the quality of malaria case management in the private sector	Malaria Care	$125,000	$0	11 states: 9 MAPS states and 2 TSHIP states	Building on pilots for Integrated Management of Childhood Illness undertaken in selected LGAs in three states in FY 2013, PMI will expand to additional states, leveraging USAID MNCH funding.
Provide support to strengthen the national drug regulatory agency's (NAFDAC) capacity	USP	$350,000	$0	Federal	Strengthen NAFDAC's capacity for drug quality control including the procurement of necessary equipment and supplies. This support will include establishing functional mini-labs that can perform key test for drug quality in the field.
Subtotal Treatment		*$11,705,000*	*$7,800,000*		
Subtotal Case Management		**$23,804,000**	**$11,800,000**		
Advocacy, Social Mobilization, and Communication					
Support a combination of BCC and social marketing	Expanded Social Marketing Program in Nigeria (ESMPIN)	$1,000,000	$0	Nationwide (with a focus in MAPS and TSHIP states)	BCC and social marketing will include intense Interpersonal Communication activities in four PMI focus states (Oyo, Zamfara, Bauchi, and Sokoto) and mass media nationwide for diagnosis and treatment of malaria, ITN ownership and use and uptake of IPTp.
Support BCC using IPC and mass media for malaria prevention, diagnosis, and treatment.	MAPS	$1,000,000	$0	9 MAPS states	BCC, using Interpersonal Communication and mass media, for malaria prevention, diagnosis and treatment through the two bilateral PMI implementing partners (MAPS and TSHIP) across the eleven focus states.
	MAPS/ Follow-on	$250,000	$0	9 MAPS states	
	TSHIP/ TBD	$150,000	$0	2 TSHIP states	
Support advocacy for malaria prevention and control	VOA	$150,000	$0	Nationwide	Advocacy for malaria prevention and control through the mass media, including working with journalists to identify and develop appropriate malaria news.
Subtotal BCC		**$2,550,000**	**$0**		

M&E					
Strengthen routine M&E systems in 11 focus states.	MAPS	$1,300,000	$0	9 MAPS states	Strengthen the harmonized HMIS at health facility, LGA, and state levels in nine MAPS and two TSHIP states. Implementation activities will include training and supervision of data clerical staff at selected health facilities, LGAs, and states; completion of unified data collection formats; and improving collection and reporting of routine malaria indicators.
	MAPS/ Follow-on	$400,000		9 MAPS states	
	TSHIP/ TBD	$210,000	$0	2 TSHIP states	
Support for FELTP.	CDC IAA	$500,000	$0	Federal	Support training for five NMCP and SMCP personnel for the two year FELTP course ($50,000/year/trainee).
TA for M&E strengthening.	CDC IAA	$24,000	$0	Federal and State level	Two CDC TDYs to provide technical support for monitoring and evaluation.
Subtotal: M&E		*$2,434,000*	*$0*		
Capacity Building					
Support to the NMCP to strengthen technical capacity and national level coordination of the malaria program.	MAPS	$500,000	0	Federal NMCP	Support for the NMCP's role as the lead coordination body through meeting support, supervision support, and training. The PMI will also provide support to eleven states to plan, implement, and monitor their malaria control programs.
Subtotal: Capacity Building		*$500,000*	*$0*		
Staffing and Administration					
In-country staffing and administration costs.	USAID/ CDC	$2,400,000	$0	Nationwide	Support for USAID and CDC annual staffing and administration costs.
Subtotal: Staffing and Administration		*$2,400,000*	*$0*		
GRAND TOTAL		**$60,100,000**	**$33,211,000**		

www.ingramcontent.com/pod-product-compliance
Lightning Source LLC
Chambersburg PA
CBHW080529290526
45790CB00006B/2349